✴ LINCOLN'S ✴ LITTLE GIRL

★ ★ ★ ★ ★ ★ ★ ★ ★ ★ ★ ★ ★ ★ ★ ★ ★ ★

A TRUE STORY

LINCOLN'S LITTLE GIRL

by FRED TRUMP

A TRUE
STORY

BOYDS MILLS PRESS

Text copyright © 1977 by Fred Trump
Jacket and interior illustrations copyright © 1993 by Boyds Mills Press
All rights reserved

Published by Bell Books
Boyds Mills Press, Inc.
A Highlights Company
815 Church Street
Honesdale, Pennsylvania 18431
Printed in the United States of America

Publisher Cataloging-in-Publication data
Trump, Fred.
   Lincoln's Little girl : a true story / by Fred Trump.
[184]p. ; cm.
Originally published by Heritage Books, Salina, Kansas, 1977.
Summary: Biography of Grace Bedell, who as a young girl wrote to Abraham
Lincoln suggesting he grow whiskers. Documented by diaries, letters, and
newspaper accounts.
ISBN 1-56397-375-8 hc / ISBN 1-56397-852-0 pbk
1. Bedell, Grace, b.1848 or 9.—Biography—Juvenile literature.
2. Lincoln, Abraham, 1809-1865—Relations with children—juvenile literature.
3.Presidents—United States—Biography—juvenile literature. [1. Bedell, Grace,
b.1848 or 9.—Biography.
2. Lincoln, Abraham, 1809-1865—Relations with children. 3. Presidents—
United States—Biography.] I. Title.
974.7'092 [B]—dc20   1993   CIP
Library of Congress catalog Card number 93-73695

First Boyds Mills Press paperback edition, 1999
Book designed by Charlie Cary
The text is set in 11-point Palatino.
Illustrations by Christopher Wray

10 9 8 7 6 5 4 3 2 1

Dedicated to

GEORGE, ROGER, AND ARTHUR BILLINGS

Grandsons of

"Lincoln's Little Girl,"
GRACE BEDELL BILLINGS

Table of Contents

Chapter 1. Stove Maker's Family
Grace Bedell, "Lincoln's little correspondent," is born in 1848 to a stove maker's family at Albion, New York.

Chapter 2. A Time of Turmoil
Grace spends her 1850s childhood as western New York's villages and hamlets are facing the turmoil of rising abolitionist sentiment, of sectional political change, of religious agitation, and of economic upheaval.

Chapter 3. A New Home at Westfield
The Bedell family moves to Westfield, New York—the earlier home of William Seward, Holland Land Grant Co. Agent, New York State governor, and Lincoln's soon-to-be Secretary of State.

Chapter 4. Presidential Campaign
Lincoln turns aside Seward's challenge for the Republican nomination in the 1860 presidential campaign.

Chapter 5. Letter to Lincoln
Grace Bedell writes to Lincoln on October 15, 1860, asking him to let his whiskers grow.

Chapter 6. Lincoln Responds
Lincoln's letter of October 19, 1860, considers the idea of whiskers for the first and last time on what has become the most famous of all American faces.

Chapter 7. Growing Whiskers
Lincoln's bearded face has come to mirror the nation's Civil War agony in the awful years of 1861-1865. Indeed, it is the face the world sees in Secretary Stanton's elegiac words: "Now he belongs to the ages."

Chapter 8. Old Abe's Kiss
Abraham Lincoln meets Miss Grace Bedell at the Westfield, New York, train depot on February 16, 1861.

Chapter 9. The Civil War
The Civil War clouds gather over western New York as eighteen-year-old George Billings of Albion, New York, is mustered into the Eighth New York Heavy Artillery Regiment.

Chapter 10. Grace and George
With the Civil War over, Grace Bedell and George Billings marry on December 3, 1867.

Chapter 11. Go West, Young Man
George Billings takes Greeley's advice to "Go west, young man, go west!" Grace waits at Albion.

Chapter 18. New Enterprises
Grace and George rejoin each other back at Delphos, Kansas, as they go on to do well in "new enterprises" other than farming.

Chapter 19. Fame Revived
Fame revisits Grace Bedell Billings when Robert Todd Lincoln's wife, Mary, finds Lincoln's letter to Grace among Robert's papers.

Chapter 20. Lincoln's Letter Sold
The avid interest in these letters shows the enduring appeal of true stories that live on whenever young people play a big role in adult affairs.

Introduction

American women were not to have the voting franchise for another sixty years when Grace Bedell, an eleven-year-old Westfield, New York, schoolgirl, impulsively wrote her famous letter to Abraham Lincoln in 1860. Her letter urging him to grow whiskers to win the notice of ladies who, in turn, would get their husbands to vote for him was surely an idea that he, as the presidential nominee of the recently formed Republican party, had not considered.

Indeed, Lincoln's great sense of humor and his uncanny understanding of children had to be instantly struck when he read Grace Bedell's letter with its sincere and certain logic.

NY
Westfield Chatauque Co
Oct. 15, 1860

Hon A B Lincoln
  Dear Sir
  My father has just home from the fair and brought home your picture and Mr. Hamlin's. I am a little girl only eleven years old, but want you should be President of the United States very much so I hope you wont think me very bold to write to, such a great man as you are. Have you any little girls about as large as I am if so give

them my love and tell her to write to me if you cannot answer this letter. I have got 4 brothers and part of them will vote for you any way, and if you will let your whiskers grow I will try and get the rest of them to vote for you you would look a great deal better for your face is so thin. All the ladies like whiskers and they would tease their husbands to vote for you and then you would be President. My father is a going to vote for you and if I was a man I would vote for you to but I will try and get every one to vote for you that I can I think that rail fence around your picture makes it look very pretty I have got a little baby sister she is nine weeks old and is just as cunning as can be. When you ~~direct~~ your letter dirct to Grace Bedell Westfield Chatauque County New York

I must not write any more answer this letter right off Good bye

Grace Bedell

Lincoln, first and foremost a writer himself, whose own words and ideas are a deep part of every freedom-loving person in the world, would know that this heartfelt letter was from a first-rate writer. When Lincoln answered it four days later, had he already decided to make such a radical change in his personal appearance? To the young at heart, it surely seems so.

Springfield, Ill. Oct. 19, 1860

Miss Grace Bedell

My dear little Miss.

Your very agreeable letter of the 15th is received.

I regret the necessity of saying I have no daughters. I have three sons—one seventeen, one nine, and one seven, years of age. They, with their mother, constitute my whole family.

As to the whiskers, having never worn any, do you not think people would call it a piece of silly affection if I were to begin it now?

Your very sincere well wisher

A. Lincoln

The people of Westfield, New York, and the surrounding villages of Chautauqua County have thought of commemorating the story of the Washington Street schoolgirl, who represents the creative energy of young people everywhere. The Grace Bedell story is a drama that takes place beyond the adult world. The story of Grace's letter and Lincoln's answer dramatizes the transcendent power of the written word itself and highlights for young people the very real excitement and possibilities in their own writing.

But here in the real world of Chautauqua County this 133-year-old event has been brought into a new community focus. Shortly after the Grace Bedell

Memorial Committee was formed in 1992, the decision was made to concentrate on Fred Trump's 1977 biography, *Lincoln's Little Girl*, which has long renewed the story's dramatic immediacy to western New York's schoolchildren, teachers, librarians, and historians. But the story surely transcends its delightful appeal beyond Westfield and Chautauqua County to the young and the young at heart everywhere. It does this in two ways: one, it emphasizes America's endless fascination with the human interest side of Lincoln; and two, it reminds us that, having studied the Lincoln-Hamlin campaign poster of 1860, Grace Bedell's intuitive conviction was right in every way. Of course, the lesson is re-affirmed that we should listen to the ideas and opinions of young people more than we do.

Trump reminds the reader that Lincoln wore the beard throughout the years of his presidency—the Civil War years. The Civil War Lincoln without the beard is just unimaginable! Indeed, simply in an inexplicable way, Lincoln's bearded face registers the tragic price to keep the Union whole: the agony of the Civil War—the 750,000 dead on both sides—is in that face, the saddest of all American faces. In fact, Lincoln's face has become the quintessential American face. It is the most easily recognized American face in the world. He is, simply, the representative American, the apotheosis of this democratic republic envisioned by Washington, Jefferson, and Madison. And with Lincoln's own anguished words faithfully enriching and bringing their "revolutionary" ideas and vocabulary through the Civil War, he makes a new declaration of independence to which each succeeding generation of free Americans must re-dedicate their sacred honor anew.

Out-of-print soon after its 1977 publication, Trump's book generated national interest in the true story of this little person who made such an inestimable difference in big people's perception of things. The memory of Fred Trump's sitting in Westfield's magnificent George W. Patterson Library, researching and writing this book in the 1970s, is one that the library staff recalls with pleasure. Mrs. Fred Trump, the author's widow, has graciously granted permission to Boyds Mills Press, publishing division of *Highlights for Children* magazine, to republish this biography. They have done this, making as few editorial changes as possible.

Mr. Trump, a Westfield, New York, native son, who spent his adult years with the U.S. Department of Agriculture in Michigan and Kansas, gives his biography two insightful directions. One is in its rural Chautauqua and Orleans County descriptions of the agricultural economy of western New York from the 1825 opening of the Erie Canal to the mounting tensions of the 1850s, and the completion of New York railroads and the post-Civil War opening of the farther West. The other is in the first eight chapters, which parallel these descriptive events with such narrative ones as Grace's marriage to George Billings at Albion, New York, at the end of the Civil War and their subsequent journey west.

From Chapter Nine through Chapter Twenty, the subject and tone remind us of Ole Rolvaag's *Giants in the Earth*—but the Kansas Territory gives us a kinder and gentler group of York State settlers than the lonely and isolated Norwegian immigrants of Rolvaag's Minnesota frontier. But life on the Kansas frontier is demanding nonetheless. So, this biography excels in the narrational events of Grace Bedell's meeting with Lincoln at the Westfield, New York, railroad station and of her subsequent life in Kansas, in the historical accuracy of its realistic descriptions of midwest farm life rivaling Hamlin Garland's, and in its earlier evocations of farm and village life in western York's Erie Canal country leading up to the Civil War.

Trump keeps Grace's point of view before the reader in evoking rural life in Westfield, New York; in fixing the location of her house on Washington Street; in being part of the crowd at the Westfield railroad station as Lincoln's train comes to a stop; in being called to come forward by the president himself; in his bending to kiss her; and in running home, still clutching her undelivered flowers. This is indeed, as the book reviewers say, "a good read" at several levels of readership.

Tristram Barnard
For The Grace Bedell Memorial Committee
Chautauqua County
at Westfield, New York

Chapter 1

STOVE MAKER'S FAMILY

On November 4, 1848, the glow of rich reds, browns, and golds in the falling autumn leaves along the streets of Albion, New York, was just beginning to fade. The maple, yellow locust, and American elm trees were nearly bare, while the oak trees were more slowly shedding their leaves. The leaden skies and crisp north wind announced that winter was just around the corner.

The spacious house at 350 West State Street in this western New York village was buzzing with excitement. Norman Bedell and his wife, Amanda, and six children already made a houseful. But in the large upstairs bedroom little Miss Grace Greenwood

Bedell burst forth into a world that was destined to feel her impact, while scarcely knowing her name.

Three days later the United States elected its second and last Whig president, General Zachary Taylor. But that event was to mean no more to Grace as a child than the election of Louis Bonaparte as president of France or the issuance of the "Communist Manifesto" by Karl Marx and Friedrich Engels that same year.

The one issue that swayed the emotions of Americans more than any other during Grace's childhood was slavery of human beings. The Bedell household was no exception. Whether slavery should be abolished or be allowed to extend into the territories was much debated within the family. Grace sided with her parents in opposing slavery, a decision that led to her appeal to the vanity of presidential candidate Abe Lincoln in 1860.

Slaveholder General Taylor won election as president, however, because of his military victory the year before in the Mexican War against General Santa Anna's superior numbers. Only the Free Soil party took a stand on slavery, while the Whigs and the Democrats avoided the issue.

Norman Bedell, born in 1805, was the older son of John Bedell, Jr., and Polly Hopkins Bedell. Polly was a Rhode Islander related to Thomas Gage, the British general whose military actions precipitated the American Revolution. The Bedells traced their lineage back to the early sixteenth century when French Huguenots named Be Delle lived at Bedell Hall, County of Essex, England.

In 1801 Norman's father purchased a rocky, hilly,

and wooded farm in an area of numerous scenic waterfalls on the southwest edge of the Adirondack Mountains in Oneida County, New York.

The family was hard-pressed to eke out a living between the boulders and granite outcrops. So in 1809 they moved west to a better farm near Marcellus, southwest of Syracuse.

Amanda Smiley Bedell, Grace's mother, was born in Herkimer County, just east of Oneida County, in 1811. Amanda's father was Dr. Francis Smiley and her mother was Eunice Mattison Smiley, a cousin of President James Madison. Amanda was an attractive and charming woman of uncompromising Methodist determination, who instilled these qualities in her children. She ran the household with what today would seem like puritanical severity.

When Norman and Amanda were married in 1827, they came west to the small Orleans County settlement that had been founded as Newport in 1811. Norman helped organize the village of Albion and built one of several early iron foundries at Albion along the Erie Canal, which had been completed in 1825.

In 1831 they purchased a new house on West State Street that was to be their home for more than forty years—except 1859 to 1861, when the family lived at Westfield, New York.

Grace's father was a stove maker by trade. In the late 1830s he went into partnership with the fatherly Richard Berry. Just before Berry's death in 1848, his 26-year-old son, Richard G. Berry, entered into a partnership with Norman Bedell, his father-in-law.

By 1851 Bedell and Berry Company had reached a

production level of twenty cast-iron cooking ranges per day at their foundry on East Bank Street paralleling the canal. The foundry employed twenty men that year. In the mid-1850s, with son George H. Bedell also as a partner, the company employed 75 to 100 men and shipped its products as far west as Detroit.

Norman possessed the tough determination needed to be successful in the industrial world of that time. It took a special kind of person to take charge in the sweaty, superheated environments of casting molten iron into stove parts.

His sons inherited their father's determined character, but did not agree among themselves or with their father on certain issues.

Norman and Amanda sought to provide their children with a good education. The Bedell home had a well-stocked library. Norman also helped found and endow Genesee Wesleyan College at Lima, New York. George Pullman, who developed the railroad sleeping car, made use of a college scholarship given by Norman Bedell.

Located halfway between Rochester and Niagara Falls and nine miles south of Lake Ontario, Albion was a thriving community during the second quarter of the nineteenth century. It depended for its livelihood upon the commerce along "the gateway to the West."

The winds of change began to be felt after the Rochester, Lockport, and Niagara Falls Railroad was built through Albion in June of 1852. The winds blew even harder when the New York Central main line came west from Rochester to Buffalo through

Batavia—fifteen miles south of Albion. The Erie Canal, however, was enlarged during the 1850s in an effort to compete with the railroads.

Many of the houses built in Albion during that period are still in use—ivy-covered, solid, red-brick houses; rambling wood-frame mansions with large rooms and still-visible interior hand-hewn timbers; and modest, one-story frame cottages.

Albion is bisected from north to south by Main Street, which runs straight uphill from the canal to the county courthouse at the center of the village. Bisecting the village from east to west is State Street.

The white clapboarded frame house at 350 West State Street is situated on the south side of the street about a block west of the site of Albion Academy,

House on West State Street, Albion, N.Y., where Grace Bedell lived most of her childhood. 1974 photo.

which Grace attended during the 1860s, and five blocks west of the courthouse. The house still stands, looking much as it did in 1848.

Although but five older Bedell children were living at the Bedell home in November of 1848, Norman and Amanda produced a total of eleven children. The eldest was Susan, born in 1831, who became Mrs. Richard G. Berry. Susan had many of her father's traits and tended to be rather bossy.

The oldest child still at home was George, 16, who was much like his father in temperament but held opposite political views. Then came even-tempered Stephen, 15. Frank, 12, was Grace's favorite among four older brothers. Levant, 11, developed political views at variance with his father's. Helen, 5, "mothered" Grace. Scott died in infancy before Grace was born. Alice, 4, had many of the gentle traits of Stephen and Grace, and was Grace's favorite sister.

After Grace came Frederick, born three years later. He was her favorite childhood playmate. The youngest, Eunice or "Una," was born in 1860.

Chapter 2

A TIME
OF TURMOIL

Grace Bedell's early childhood during the 1850s was a time of national turmoil that unconsciously shaped her life. The harsh treatment of slaves described in Harriet Beecher Stowe's book *Uncle Tom's Cabin* touched Grace's heart, as it did the hearts of her mother and sisters.

As a very young child, Grace couldn't understand how underground railroad tunnels could be dug all the way from the South to the North without being discovered. Later she learned that "underground railroad" was a figurative term applied to the clandestine movement of runaway slaves above ground from the South to the Canadian border.

Everyone in Albion, including Grace, knew that the tavern at Barre Center, four miles south of Albion, was a way station on the underground railroad. It was also common knowledge that the Erie Canal itself was used to transport fleeing slaves.

Feelings in the community were divided, however, on the question of helping fugitive slaves. Some people held to the principle that the fugitive slave law should be obeyed because it was the law of the land. But few people dared report runaway slaves, for anti-slavery feelings ran high.

Millard Fillmore, president of the United States from 1850 to 1853, was opposed to slavery personally, but enforced the fugitive slave law in order to hold the nation together.

His successor, Franklin Pierce, also attempted to hold the Union together. But acting upon the advice of Democratic party leaders, he signed into law Senator Stephen Douglas's Kansas-Nebraska Bill in 1854. The law provided that the people in the two new territories would decide for themselves whether or not to permit slavery.

Grace's first recollections of the word "Kansas"— her home for nearly all of her adult life—were associated with the civil war that took place in Kansas Territory between pro-slavery and anti-slavery groups during the 1850s. She imagined that the soil in "bleeding Kansas" was stained red with blood.

Douglas's bill also helped unravel the Whig party, polarizing anti-slavery elements into the new Republican party. The whole nation, in fact, was becoming more and more polarized on the issue of slavery. The South, according to Grace's father, seemed to be going to new extremes to morally justify slavery.

One of the most influential men in America during Grace's childhood was Horace Greeley, editor of the *New York Tribune*. In 1854 he launched an editorial campaign that rallied the North to stop the extension of slavery. He named a new and growing faction "Republicans."

Thus in 1856 the Republicans became the first major political party to take a stand against slavery, while the Democrats continued to appeal to conservatives with the position that to compromise on the slavery issue was to preserve the Union. Fillmore's Know-Nothing party cut into the vote for the Republican party's first presidential candidate, John C. Fremont. Democrat James Buchanan was elected president. What many Albionites regarded as the "inevitable conflict" was delayed.

As a result of a series of debates in Illinois with Douglas in 1858, the name of the new and effective spokesman against the extension of slavery came into the consciousness of upstate New Yorkers. That man was Abraham Lincoln.

Little Grace Bedell lived a normal childhood, in spite of the overtones of the slavery issue on everyone's mind. "Going somewhere" in her early years meant going shopping with her mother on Bank Street, or the familiar walk up State Street to the Methodist-Episcopal church near the courthouse. Her father had been a trustee of the church before she was born.

She was never permitted to go near the canal by herself, or to go to the fair, or to enter her father's foundry. She, like the other children, often waved to the canal boat captains from a safe distance. The boat horns were always tooted in response.

She regarded with awe the changing seasons—the bright colors of autumn leaves, the intriguing piles of leaves on the ground, the pure white of newfallen snow, the soupy slush of winter thaws, the first flowers of spring, the explosion of new leaves on the trees, and the altogether pleasant days of summer.

One Sunday in the spring of 1857, when Grace was eight years old, she listened to the preacher describe the Devil's temptation. Verses 5 through 7 of the fourth chapter of Matthew puzzled Grace.

> Then the devil taketh him into the holy city;
> and he set him on the pinnacle of the temple,
> and saith unto him: If thou art the Son of God,
> cast thyself down; for it is written,
> He shall give his angels charge
> concerning thee and
> On their hands they shall bear thee up,
> Lest haply thou dash thy foot
> against a stone.
> Jesus said unto him: Again it is written,
> Thou shalt not make trial of the Lord thy God.

On the way home from church Grace looked up to her mother and asked, "Mother, is it true that God's angels will lift me up and keep me from being hurt if I should fall?" Grace envisioned a shining, golden-winged figure suddenly appearing—a wonderful sight she had never seen, except in pictures.

Her mother replied casually, "Why, of course He

will, Gracie dear." Amanda thought no more of the conversation and went on with the preparation of dinner for the family.

But Grace could not get those golden angels out of her mind. When no one was looking she ran upstairs, opened the low window at the top of the stairs, and walked onto the porch roof. Then she jumped off the roof into the front yard. She broke both legs!

As she grew up Grace developed a wholesome, optimistic attitude toward life and maintained her belief in God. But the puritanical organized church as she knew it did not appeal to her. She also became extremely wary of how the Bible was interpreted.

Like the rest of the community and the nation, the First Methodist-Episcopal Church of Albion was caught up in the slavery issue during the late 1850s. By 1859 the church was in deep financial trouble due to internal discord over slavery. In 1859 the Reverend Loren Stiles, Jr., was expelled from the church for his fiery abolitionist views and for other doctrinal differences. The church split in two as 185 members of the congregation followed him to organize the First Congregational Free Methodist Church of Albion— the first church of this denomination in the United States.

The turmoil within the Methodist Church in Albion caused much argument within the Bedell family, too. Grace's father was swayed by Stiles and was tempted to follow him to his meetings at the nearby academy. Her brother, George, then 27, was violently opposed to Stiles's actions and supported his expulsion. His strict wife, Amelia, backed him. So did his brother, Levant, 22. Amanda tried to make peace within the family. The net result was that throughout 1859, Grace, her parents, her sisters, and her younger brother almost stopped going to church. Grace didn't know what to think about church politics. All she knew was that it wasn't right to keep any human being in slavery.

Finally, her father saw a way to get out of his family's dilemma and to meet a new employment opportunity at the same time.

It was with a sense of relief and anticipation that the decision was made to move to Westfield, New York, a village sixty-five miles southwest of Buffalo in Chautauqua County. Here Grace's father had an opportunity to extend his stove-making knowledge and experience to a large stove works along Chautauqua Creek. He left son George and son-in-law Richard in charge of the company in Albion.

Thus in October of 1859, just before Grace's eleventh birthday, the Bedells rented out their house, packed their trunks, and traveled by train to Buffalo and then on to Westfield. Making the move with Grace were her parents, as well as Helen, Alice, Levant, Frederick, Stephen and his wife, Lucy, and their baby daughter.

Chapter 3

A NEW HOME AT WESTFIELD

The name "Westfield" sounded "out west" to Grace. She was thus surprised to come upon a village of some three thousand people that was similar to Albion in many ways. Instead of being "out west," Westfield was a gateway to the West at the western tip of New York State on a narrow corridor of lake plain between the Allegheny Plateau and Lake Erie.

Her father rented a house owned by Alfred Couch at 36 Washington Street, two blocks from the Buffalo and Erie Railroad depot. So it was a short ride with their trunks by wagon south on Franklin Street, across Jefferson Street, and up a slight grade to Washington Street. A left turn on Washington Street, paralleling the railroad tracks, brought them to the unassuming cottage that was to be their home.

Like the Bedell house at Albion, the Bedell house at Westfield is still occupied, looking much as it did in 1859. Their new home was older than their house at Albion, having been built in 1821. Today the house is one of the oldest in Westfield, which has scores of houses dating from before the Civil War.

Washington Street was graced with several large houses, some still standing. One mansion three lots east of the Bedells was occupied by Alvin Plumb, president of the Westfield Academy. Across the street from the Plumb house was the many-gabled home of Henry Kingsbury, the county's leading attorney.

Grace was the only member of the family to occupy a bedroom of her own. It was the smallest bedroom, located at the rear of the second floor, with a window looking out onto the backyard.

As Christmas approached, Grace became aware that snowfalls were heavier than at Albion. Before Lake Erie freezes over, usually about January 1, cold winter winds sweep across the warmer waters of the lake, picking up large quantities of moisture and depositing it as snow and rain on the southeast shore. The plateau, rising about five hundred feet in elevation two miles south of the village, accentuates this phenomenon. During that snowy winter, Grace had to walk west past only two houses to reach the plain schoolhouse, set well back from the street.

It was also a short walk for Grace and her family on gravel sidewalks to the Methodist church—a block west on their street and south for a block on North Portage Street to Clinton Street. The church stood on

The Bedell house on Washington Street, Westfield, N.Y., where Grace Bedell wrote her famous letter to Lincoln. 1974 photo.

the north side of Clinton Street, with one house between it and North Portage.

Three houses east of the church was the home of Thomas Macomber, a carriage and sleigh maker and one of the community's most ardent abolitionists. Jennie, his daughter, was one of Grace's acquaintances.

It was one more block south on North Portage to the intersection with Main Street, where the Westfield House, a hotel with a broad veranda, stood at the northwest corner of "The Crossroads." The village park occupied the opposite corner. South Portage and Main streets, two churches, and the village's first framed house (built by pioneer settler James McClurg) surrounded the park. Shops lined the two brick streets next to the park.

The main road east and west out of Westfield followed an Indian trail along a gravel ridge that had marked the lake shore during the Ice Age. Grace could see the upward slope of the ridge as she looked outside from her south bedroom window.

Just west of the Portage Streets was a bluff that dropped sharply to Chautauqua Creek valley. During the latter part of the Ice Age the creek was a sluggish, meandering stream. But as the ice melted and the lake level dropped, the stream cut a deep gorge.

On a level area behind the Westfield House, between the bluff and the creek and along a bend in the creek, was located the Townsend Manufacturing Company. This was an extensive stove-making operation that included malleable iron ovens, a brass foundry, and Japan ovens. A sluice for water power bisected the curve. Norman Bedell had a supervisory position in the office located just below the hotel.

Next to the hotel on North Portage Street was Macomber's carriage-making shop. Also nearby was a livery stable operated by Grace's brothers Frank and Stephen. Frank had quit his printer's job at Crown Point, Indiana, and had come back east with his wife, Leila. Her father was Solon Robinson, a founder of Crown Point and during the Civil War an associate editor under Horace Greeley on the *New York Tribune.*

In the fall of 1860, the *Westfield Republican* carried this advertisement:

Bedell and Brother's carriages, with
careful drivers furnished on short notice.
Stables at Westfield House.

William Seward, the hook-nosed political leader

who almost had the presidency within his grasp in 1860, came to Westfield in 1836 as the agent of the Holland Land Company. He succeeded in soothing the tempers of landholders who had burned the land office the year before at the nearby county seat of Mayville. At first he lived in the McClurg house, and later in a majestic mansion that Grace could see to her right as she turned the corner at Washington and North Portage streets.

When Seward was elected governor of New York in 1838, the Big Whig was succeeded as land agent by George W. Patterson. Ten years later Patterson, who lived in the Seward house, was elected lieutenant governor of New York. When Grace lived at Westfield, Patterson was called "Governor" and was the community's most prominent citizen.

Horace Greeley was well known in the area; and he knew the area well, too, having worked in and around the county as a journeyman printer at the ages of nineteen and twenty in 1830 and 1831. At that time his parents lived in a Pennsylvania wilderness cabin forty-five miles south of Westfield. Several times Greeley walked alone across a Chautauqua County wilderness abounding in wolves and bears, but devoid of Indians. Greeley occasionally visited Westfield later in life, for his sociable and outgoing sister, Mrs. Esther Cleveland, lived there. Esther also lived at Greeley's home for a time, attempting to create a social life for the famous editor that his mentally ill wife was unable to do.

For most of his long and distinguished career Greeley was the foremost spokesman of Manifest Destiny, urging large numbers of people to settle up the West. "Go west, young man" was his well-known slogan. Early in his career as a newspaperman in New York City, beginning in 1831, the "west" in which he urged his readers to settle was Chautauqua County, New York, and adjacent Erie County, Pennsylvania.

Early in 1855, as the Whig party crumbled to dust, Patterson called a secret meeting of Whig political leaders at Mayville to form the Republican Party in New York State. The meeting site was chosen because it was remote from prying eyes and ears (including newspaper reporters) at the state capital at Albany, and because two of the leading Whigs present, Greeley and Seward, knew the area. Attending from Westfield were Austin Smith, attorney, state assemblyman, and principal of Fredonia Academy; his partner, State Senator Abram Dixon; the Bedells' neighbor, Alvin Plumb; and the banker Sextus Hungerford. The banker occupied a large mansion and estate on North Portage Street nearly opposite the Patterson house. (In the spring of 1860 Hungerford acquired ownership of the house where the Bedells lived.)

Following the Mayville meeting, the group met at Westfield and prevailed upon attorney Martin Rice to become editor of the *Westfield Republican*, the nation's first organ of the Republican party. The first issue was printed April 25, 1855.

Thus it was with great interest that the citizens of Westfield followed the fateful events within the Republican party leading up to the presidential election of 1860.

Chapter 4

PRESIDENTIAL CAMPAIGN

When the Republican national convention convened at Chicago on May 16, 1860, former Westfieldite William Seward was so confident he would receive the nomination on the first ballot—and eventually be elected president—that he had a cannon placed on the lawn of his home at Auburn, New York. The cannon was to be fired as soon as the telegraph brought the news of his nomination.

Seward symbolized the wealth, culture, and power of the East. But powerful forces opposed him. One who mistrusted him was editor Horace Greeley, who had been a political associate for over twenty-five years. In March, 1860, Greeley came out publicly against Seward. For president, Greeley favored Edward Bates of Missouri, who later served as Lincoln's attorney general.

A typical Western view of Seward and Stephen Douglas, the leading Democrat, was expressed in the January 11, 1860, issue of the *Weekly Illinois State Journal* published at Springfield:

> We cannot countenance Seward, because he is a scoundrel and avows it. We cannot countenance Douglas, because he is a scoundrel and denies it.

Another reemerging force throughout 1859 and 1860 was a gangling, six-foot-four scarecrow of a man from Springfield named Abraham Lincoln. He had come into national prominence during a losing senatorial race against that five-foot-four "little giant," Stephen Douglas.

"Lincoln has had no experience in national politics," declared Greeley in a myopic moment.

Perhaps the most crucial event of the entire political campaign of 1860 was Lincoln's address at the Cooper Union, between Fourth Avenue and Eighth Street in New York City, on February 27. A raging snowstorm limited his audience to fifteen hundred people. But what he said and how he said it probably swung more voters toward him than anything else he did that year.

Before he made his first trip to the big city, Lincoln had established a wide reputation for his witty anecdotes and his backwoods stories, and for his skill as a frontier lawyer. But as president? Questionable.

His high cheekbones, large ears, extraordinarily long arms and legs, big feet, and the large mole on his right cheek made him the subject of caricature and ridicule in the East. His normal speaking voice was shrill and piercing. But when he sought to make an impression, it became soft, smooth, musical, and convincing. The Cooper Union speech was such an occasion.

His speech was a masterpiece of logic as he explored, one by one, the views on the subject of slavery of each signer of the Constitution. The consensus was that slavery is an evil that must not be extended to areas where it has not existed before, but that slavery should be permitted where it already exists. This was Lincoln's stand, and his listeners understood that therein lay the path to a Republican victory in November. Seward, Beecher, and others, on the other hand, advocated abolition of slavery throughout the nation.

Of Lincoln's speech, the *New York Tribune* said:

No man ever made such an impression on his first appeal to a New York audience.

The choice of Chicago as the location for the Republican convention was a stroke of good fortune for the Lincoln forces. On May 17 enthusiastic Seward supporters marched too long in the streets. When they returned to "The Wigwam," a temporary wooden building serving as the convention center, they found no vacant seats. Lincoln's managers had printed duplicate seat tickets and distributed them to Illinois supporters of Lincoln.

As expected, Seward led on the first ballot with 173½ votes to Lincoln's 102. It required 233 votes for a majority. Lincoln narrowed the gap to 181, while Seward led with 184½ on the second ballot. Lincoln received the nomination on the third ballot. To many people his nomination was a triumph of the people over the politicians.

The Republican platform prohibited slavery in the territories, supported a homestead act, and favored defense of the Union. The platform disavowed the anti-slavery insurrection tactics of John Brown's supporters. Greeley and Beecher, on the other hand, suggested that the slave states should leave the Union in peace.

Prior to the Republican convention, the Democrats had met at Charleston, S.C., but failed to nominate a candidate. Southern delegates demanded that the Democratic party advocate the extension of slavery. Douglas, the leading candidate, could not agree to those terms. When the Democrats convened again at Baltimore after the Republican convention, Douglas received the nomination—but only after the Southern delegates had walked out. Southern Democrats nominated Vice-President John C. Breckinridge of Kentucky as their presidential candidate. The split almost guaranteed Lincoln's election, especially when President James Buchanan, a Democrat, refused to support Douglas. A group of older conservatives added further to the splintering by forming the Constitutional Union party and nominating sixty-three-year-old John Bell of Tennessee for president. His backers felt that the election of any of the others would tear the nation asunder.

Lincoln remained at Springfield during the convention and throughout the campaign, as was the custom at that time. It was not considered dignified for a candidate to stump the country on his own behalf. Lincoln made no campaign speeches that summer, for he felt that his earlier speeches and the party platform said what he wanted to say. The candidate, however, did make occasional informal remarks before groups of well-wishers at Springfield. He received scores of letters a week, sometimes as many as fifty a day. The visitors and letter writers included newsmen, office seekers, job seekers, photographers, painters, and people offering and seeking political advice. Many of them abused Lincoln's patience, but he remained calm throughout the whole ordeal.

Although he did not travel about during the campaign, he followed events closely and was quick with advice for campaign workers, including Thurlow Weed, New York party boss, and Hannibal Hamlin of Maine, his vice-presidential running mate.

The letter Grace Bedell wrote to Lincoln on October 15, 1860 is in the Burton Collection at the Detroit Public Library.

Chapter 5

LETTER TO LINCOLN

The presidential campaign during the summer and fall of 1860 aroused such excitement throughout the nation and at Westfield that eleven-year-old Grace Bedell was also caught up in the emotions of the time.

Only once during those weeks did another exciting event overshadow the campaign in the Bedell household. That was in August when baby sister Eunice was born. Eunice "Una" Madison Bedell, named for her grandmother and Grandma's cousin, President Madison, became a great favorite of Grace's.

Excitement was rekindled every time Lincoln supporters, called "The Wide-Awake Boys," paraded in the streets. They wore black enameled "oilcloth" capes with white trim and the name of their group lettered in white on the capes. Black, glazed caps matched the capes. As they marched, they sang:

O, Abe Lincoln came out of the wilderness
Out of the wilderness,
Out of the wilderness.
Old Abe Lincoln came out of the wilderness
   down in Illinois.

Grace observed some of these evening parades that were lighted with torches and barrels of pungent, burning tar. Likenesses of Lincoln and Hamlin were carried aloft on banners, but Grace never got a good look at Lincoln's face, except with shadows upon it.

Widely displayed during the 1860 campaign were posters and broadsides that accentuated Lincoln's thin face and gave him an emaciated appearance. Thick, heavy-featured Hamlin's face beside it was a marked contrast.

Although Westfield was largely Republican in sentiment, Grace was impressed with how vocal local Democrats were. Many of the working men employed with her father were Douglas Democrats.

In later years Grace was asked many times to recall the events of late 1860 and early 1861. Here is one quote:

The other children would compare Mr. Lincoln with Douglas and would make fun of Mr. Lincoln, saying he was ugly and no good. They also wrote mean rhymes about him.

We had many arguments in school about
the various candidates' merits. Nearly all
children believe as their parents believe. I
thought he was handsome until I saw his
picture.

Grace's parents were ardent Lincoln supporters, as
were her brothers Frank and Stephen, both of voting
age. There were many political discussions within the
Bedell household that summer and fall, especially
when her brother George came to visit from Albion.
George and Levant both planned to vote for Douglas.
George teased Grace because she became so
emotional in her support for Lincoln.

The matter came to a head when Westfield held
its first annual village fair, sponsored by the
Metropolitan Fairground Association, on Wednesday
through Friday, October 10 to 12, at the south edge of
town. Norman Bedell went to the fair and brought
home one of the Republican campaign posters, a 28-
by 36-inch broadside called "The National Republican
Charts." Around the edges of the poster were
grouped the pictures of the former presidents, while
in the center were the larger faces of Lincoln and
Hamlin, surrounded by a rail fence signifying
Lincoln's humble, frontier upbringing. (One of these
posters, valued at $500, is now in the possession of
the Lincoln National Life Foundation of Fort Wayne,
Indiana.)

"A glance at the huge and gaudy poster brought to
us children by our father was rather disappointing,"
Grace related years later.

The poster picture of Lincoln was based upon a

Republican campaign poster

44

painting done by New York City artist Thomas Hicks at Springfield on June 12 and 13, 1860. It was the first oil portrait ever made of Lincoln, and it greatly improved upon his natural appearance. Mrs. Lincoln's reaction to the painting, however, was, "Yes, that is Mr. Lincoln. It is exactly like him." (The painting sold for $11,000 in 1940.)

If Grace thought that the poster picture made Lincoln look homely, she should have seen the actual photographs of the clean-shaven Lincoln. One photograph of Lincoln, taken in June, 1860, by William Shaw, made Lincoln appear particularly unhandsome.

Grace studied the face on the Lincoln poster. She admired the noble brow and the fine eyes. But the lower part of the angular features with deeply chiseled lines about the mouth disturbed her.

One of the most descriptive accounts of the events in Grace Bedell's life leading up to her writing a letter to Lincoln is found in part of an article written by her husband's reporter nephew, Charles Stilson, Jr., in the February 12, 1928, issue of the *Democrat-Chronicle*, Rochester, New York:

In 1860 the nomination to the presidency
of the United States went to a tall, middle-
aged lawyer of Sangamon County, Illinois.
His friends believed him to be a strong
nominee. The rest of the country wondered.
It had need of a strong man; for with the
nomination, Abraham Lincoln voluntarily and
with foreknowledge shouldered that black and
shadowy casket freighted with all the

miseries of Pandora—and when it remembers to look back, the world still wonders at the power and patience with which he bore it.

Among these memories so much is tragic and gloomy that a glint of kindly humor is as precious as gold in a mine. Lincoln himself created many such a gleam. Somewhere in a corner of his mind lived a whimsical little boy who refused to grow up, and he often came out to play on the dullest and most solemn occasions. He was mischievous, but never malicious, and he didn't care a cent for the most forbidding frown. One of the brightest fragments of Lincoln's life concerns this prankish sprite and Grace Bedell.

Grace Bedell was eleven years old in 1860 when Lincoln was nominated. She lived with her parents in Westfield, where they had moved the year before from Albion. Grace was a hero worshipper, romantic—sentimental, if you will—a sincere deeply feeling mother's girl child.

Of the politicians who went into that far-off campaign, Grace selected Lincoln as her hero; to him she attached her girlish fancy, and she would hear no ill of him without protest.

Many persons ridiculed Lincoln, those of them who found no fault with his policies picking on his personal appearance.

"Uncouth," some of the jesters called the child's idol; "backwoodsman," "raw-boned rail-splitter," "awkward," "homely as a hedge fence."

Grace's sensitive idealism rebelled against these rude epithets, and she replied with spirit; even her parents smiled at the vigor of her defense.

With the prescience that is the property of imaginative children, it was the inner man she saw, and not his garment. A multitude that had been blind saw him later.

So many tongues against one child were heavy odds. They forced her to conclude there must be something in her talk. Her father had brought home one of the current campaign posters that bore the portraits of Lincoln and Hamlin. Grace studied with care the large, deeply graven lines of Lincoln's face.

After courageously facing the fact, womanlike, she sought the remedy. At length she thought she had discovered it.

After much fanciful trying on of this and that imaginary alteration, she one day said to her mother:

"I think that Mr. Lincoln might look much nicer if he wore whiskers."

She had vision in Lincoln's face as the world knows it—the craglike nose and jutting chin, those salient cheekbones, beetling brows, and heavy lips, framed in softening, toning growth of beard—the word in those days was whiskers.

Her remedy found, nothing would do the little woman but she must try to apply it. Her determination—compound of sincerity,

childish simplicity, and the spirit of
adventurous romance that touches with rare
colors the everyday drabness of life—led
her to sit down and write to Mr. Lincoln.

In 1878 Grace wrote to John Carroll Powers,
custodian of the Lincoln Monument at Springfield:

We were at that time residing at Westfield, New York. My father, who was a
staunch Republican, brought one day to me—
who followed in his footsteps and was a
zealous champion of Mr. Lincoln—a picture
of Lincoln and Hamlin, one of those coarse,
exaggerated likenesses which it seems the
fate of our long-suffering people. You are
familiar with Mr. Lincoln's physiognomy, and
remember the high forehead over those sadly
pathetic eyes, the angular lower face with
the deep cut lines about the mouth.
I proceeded to write to him my name,
age, place of residence, my views of his
fitness for the presidency, opinion of his
personal appearance, and that I thought it
would be much improved if he would cultivate
whiskers, adding, as an inducement, that if he
would I would try my best to coax my two Democratic brothers to cast their votes for him. In
my heart of heart I feared that this rather free
criticism might give offense, and so tried to
soften the blow by assuring him that I
thought the rail fence around his picture
looked really pretty, and ended by asking him

if he had no time to answer my letter to
allow his little girl to reply for him.

Grace thought of nothing else the entire weekend
following the fair, as the idea churned and then jelled
in her mind. While thinking about whiskers, she
remembered the shadows on his picture during the
torchlight parades.

So after school on Monday, October 15, she hurried
to the privacy of her own bedroom, gazed out into the
backyard deep in thought, and then carefully penned
the famous letter to Lincoln.

Among other errors in the letter, she misspelled
Chautauqua, left out the word "come" in the first
sentence, omitted some punctuation, and inadvertently crossed out the word "direct" once near
the end of the letter. She also spelled "Abe" as "A B."
The wording of the letter follows:

NY
Westfield Chatauque Co
Oct. 15, 1860

Hon A B Lincoln
  Dear Sir
    My father has just home from the fair
and brought home your picture and Mr.
Hamlin's. I am a little girl only eleven
years old, but want you should be President
of the United States very much so I hope you
wont think me very bold to write to, such a
great man as you are. Have you any little
girls about as large as I am if so give them

my love and tell her to write to me if you cannot answer this letter. I have got 4 brothers and part of them will vote for you any way, and if you will let your whiskers grow I will try and get the rest of them to vote for you you would look a great deal better for your face is so thin. All the ladies like whiskers and they would tease their husbands to vote for you and then you would be President. My father is a going to vote for you and if I was a man I would vote for you to but I will try and get every one to vote for you that I can I think that rail fence around your picture makes it look very pretty I have got a little baby sister she is nine weeks old and is just as cunning as can be. When you ~~direct~~ your letter dirct to Grace Bedell Westfield Chatauque County New York

I must not write any more answer this letter right off Good bye

Grace Bedell

She had little time to reflect upon her bold deed, as she quickly addressed the envelope and affixed a penny stamp. She had to make a secret trip to the post office on Main Street before supper.

She didn't really expect that he himself, important man that he was, would personally answer her letter.

Chapter 6

LINCOLN RESPONDS

Over the centuries beards have been an issue of heated controversy. Beards have come into and gone out of fashion in regular cycles. Whenever they were in fashion, beards were considered a symbol of virility and "male superiority." Whenever beards were out of fashion among Gentiles during the Middle Ages, persecution of bearded Jews took an upturn. A century after Lincoln's presidency, beards again became a controversial issue.

During the 1850s beards and mustaches were worn by many men in the United States. But most men of fashion were clean-shaven. In pioneer days the course of least resistance encouraged most men on the frontier to grow beards. Frontiersman Thomas Lincoln was always clean-shaven, however, and Abe had followed his father's example.

Lincoln, of course, was aware that his enemies were poking fun at his ungainly form and thin features, and that cartoonists found him an easy subject to caricature. He had no illusions about his appearance.

Grace was not the only one to suggest to Lincoln that he grow whiskers. Some influential political leaders in the Republican party advised him to grow a beard to give him a look of distinction. About the time Grace was writing her letter, Lincoln received this letter:

October 12, 1860

To the Hon. Abm. Lincoln

Dear Sir
    Allow a number of very earnest
Republicans to intimate to you that after
oft-repeated views of the daguerrotypes,
which we wear as tokens of our devotedness to
you, we have come to the candid determination
that these medals would be much improved in
appearance provided you would cultivate
whiskers and wear standing collars.
    Believe us nothing but an earnest desire
that "our candidate" should be the best
looking as well as the best of the rival
candidates, would induce us to trespass upon

your valued time.
Your most sincere and earnest well wishers
True Republicans
P.S. We really fear votes will be lost to
"the cause" unless our "gentle hints" are
attended to.   T.R.

When Lincoln received this letter, it is likely that he neither accepted nor rejected the idea of a beard.

It is remarkable that Grace's letter to Lincoln got past Lincoln's efficient secretary, John Nicolay, and assistant secretary, John Hay, for they answered most of the candidate's letters. Perhaps Hay, being only twenty-two years old, made a point to have the child's letter come to Lincoln's personal attention. Later, following Lincoln's example, Nicolay himself grew a long beard, while Hay produced a large mustache.

Lincoln was amused—and moved—by the little girl's letter. It was said of him that "he couldn't refuse a child anything." It was very much in character for the big-hearted Illinoisan to ponder over this childish suggestion, instead of ignoring it as a silly impertinence.

Lincoln was so touched by Grace's appeal that he committed a Freudian slip when he wrote "affection" instead of "affectation." Lincoln had a special fondness for little girls and regretted very much that he had none of his own. The Lincoln family was saddened by the loss of three of their four sons during their youth. The sons Lincoln wrote about in his reply to Grace were Robert, the eldest, who grew up to become Secretary of War, Minister to England,

and president of the Pullman Company; Thomas "Tad," who died in 1871 at the age of eighteen; and Willie, who died in the White House at the age of eleven early in 1862. Another son, Edward, had died ten years earlier at the age of four.

On Friday Lincoln personally answered Grace's letter:

<u>Private</u>

Springfield, Ill. Oct. 19, 1860

Miss Grace Bedell
  My dear little Miss.
    Your very agreeable letter of the 15th
is received.
    I regret the necessity of saying I have
no daughters. I have three sons—one
seventeen, one nine, and one seven, years of
age. They, with their mother, constitute my
whole family.
    As to the whiskers, having never worn
any, do you not think people would call it a
piece of silly affection if I were to begin
it now?

Your very sincere well wisher
A. Lincoln

Historian William E. Barton has given this account of Lincoln's reaction:

Almost from the very day of her letter,
he decided he would wear a beard. He would
have done so if he had had a little daughter

and she had asked him to do so; and he did it at this little girl's request.

Perhaps this is as strange a story as can be truthfully related of any President or presidential candidate in the history of the United States—that he consented to so radical a change in his personal appearance at the suggestion of a little girl.

All the portraits taken in Springfield and Chicago had been beardless; and the Brady photographs made in New York when Lincoln was there to deliver his Cooper Union address had come to be recognized throughout the country.

So far as is known, no Senator or Governor or prospective cabinet member told Mr. Lincoln that he ought to wear a beard, but he gave the matter serious consideration when a little girl wrote and suggested it.

It was Monday, October 22, a week after Grace had written to Lincoln, when she stopped at the Westfield post office. To her great surprise and excitement Postmaster David Mann handed her a letter addressed to her—marked "Private." Many years later Grace gave this account:

My people didn't know I had written to Mr. Lincoln. When I received the one from him, I opened it to read on my way home. A slight skiff of snow was falling, but it was hardly cold enough for snow, and it melted as it fell.

Pointing to the Lincoln letter, and refuting the tale that she cried tears upon the letter, she continued.

You'll see many brown spots on it, like
big freckles. That's where flakes of snow
fell on it as a very excited little girl was
trying to read a letter and run home as fast
as she could at the same time.
    I rushed in upon my mother and two or
three sisters. All were very much surprised.
My sister Helen asked me how I knew where to
address the letter. I replied that I read in
the paper that Mr. Lincoln lived at
Springfield, Illinois. They all laughed.
Then Helen asked, "How did you address your
letter?"
    I told her, "Hon. Abraham Lincoln,
Esquire." They all laughed again. But
Mother spoke up and said, "Well, I guess he
received the letter all right. The
postmaster at Springfield would be in no
doubt for whom the letter was intended."

(Recalling the incident many years later, she did not remember the salutation correctly.)

Grace's mother then remembered that Grace had earlier expressed the idea of whiskers for Lincoln, and the incident of Grace's broken legs came to mind. She said to herself, "I must pay more attention to what Grace is saying."

Grace's heart pounded with excitement as she lay on her bed reading the letter over and over again. But she frowned as she read Lincoln's last sentence. He

Grace Greenwood Bedell, 14, Albion, N.Y., 1863.

called whiskers "a silly piece of affection." At first she didn't catch the distinction between "affection" and "affectation," but she had a general understanding of what he was saying. She concluded that her hero was telling her that he would not grow whiskers.

The news of a letter from Lincoln went around the village, and a number of people stopped by the Bedell home to see the letter. Their neighbors, Mr. and Mrs. Alvin Plumb, were among the first to read the letter, since Mr. Plumb had been one of the founders of the New York Republican party. Grace, of course, took the letter to school to show to her teacher and the other children. But the incident was not reported in the *Westfield Republican*. The letter was soon forgotten outside the Bedell family. Grace lay on her bed and read the letter every evening until the news came that Lincoln had been elected president of the United States.

Grace's Democratic brothers remained faithful to their party, in spite of her efforts, although they privately conceded that Lincoln would be elected. Even Democrats encountering Lincoln in Illinois late in the campaign inadvertently addressed him as "Mr. President."

On the evening of Tuesday, November 6, 1860, Election Day, Grace, now twelve, was assured by her father and her Republican brothers that they had indeed voted for Lincoln. Rumors floated about the village the next day from telegraph reports that Lincoln was indeed winning the election.

The election was close. Lincoln's final total popular vote was 1,866,452. Douglas received 1,376,957;

Breckinridge 849,781; and Bell 588,879. Lincoln's total electoral vote was 180. He carried every free state, but not a single southern state. Douglas carried only Missouri. For several days the outcome in New Jersey was in doubt. Lincoln finally took four electoral votes and Douglas three from that state. Secessionist Breckinridge carried the entire South, with 72 electoral votes. Douglas received 12 electoral votes and Bell 39.

Breckinridge went on to become a successful Confederate general. Like Jefferson Davis and Sam Houston in their home states, Bell pleaded in vain in 1861 to keep his native Tennessee from seceding. Douglas offered his services to Lincoln to help preserve the Union. The Little Giant was sent into the border states on a public relations tour that was cut short by his untimely death.

The South hated Lincoln with a consuming passion. Assassination was spoken of as a real possibility, even probability. The southern states were only waiting for a good excuse to secede. When Lincoln won the election, they felt the time was ripe. They acted, thinking that the northern states would not go to war against them.

South Carolina was the first state to secede—on December 20, 1860. During the next month Mississippi, Florida, Alabama, Georgia, and Louisiana followed suit. These six states then organized the Confederate States of America in February, 1861. President Buchanan, however, refused to take any military action against the secessionist states. Texas seceded in March when Lincoln was inaugurated. The new Secretary of State, William

Seward, even suggested provoking a war with a European power in an attempt to unite the entire nation, including the South. Lincoln ignored Seward's advice.

The war that everyone dreaded began at 4:30 a.m. on Friday, April 12, 1861, when southern troops bombarded Fort Sumter in Charleston harbor. When this overt military action took place against the Union, Virginia, Tennessee, Arkansas, and North Carolina also seceded. Eleven Confederate states faced twenty-three Union states.

This was Lincoln's letter of response to Grace Bedell.

Chapter 7

GROWING
WHISKERS

Late in October of 1860 Lincoln said to his barber, as he was about to be shaved, "Billy, let's give them a chance to grow." The latest photograph of Lincoln, one taken by Preston Butler at Springfield on August 13, 1860, now became obsolete. On Sunday, November 25, 1860, Samuel G. Alschuler of Chicago made the first bearded photograph of Lincoln. It was a peculiar, scrubby, half-beard, quite different from the fully-bearded Lincoln face that the world later remembered him by.

The next day the *New York Herald* reported:

On Sunday Lincoln and Hamlin attended

church. Lincoln also sat for a photographer, the result being a unique half-bearded portrait.

On December 27 this item appeared in the *Daily Journal* of Evansville, Indiana:

> They say that Old Abe is raising a pair of whiskers. Some individual of the cockney persuasion remarked that he was "a puttin' on (h)airs."

In the late weeks of 1860 and early 1861 nearly everyone was talking about the "noble hirsute appendage" the president-elect had affected. Those close to Lincoln in the Republican party were quick to point out that bearded men of action were now destined to take over the reins of government from clean-shaven men who dressed in broadcloth and whose chief attribute was oratory.

The opposition press made fun of the beard. The Bedells even found in the *Orleans Republican* of Albion in February, 1861, this item:

> There seems to be something supremely ridiculous in these troubled times, when our very national existence is imperiled, in having a President-elect who devotes his energies to cultivating whiskers and otherwise improving his personal appearance.

Grace was elated to learn that Lincoln was growing a beard, and she certainly shared this newspaper's concern about the troubled times. But she was disappointed that the editor disapproved of "her" beard. The editor undoubtedly did not know that an Albion native had suggested the beard.

Two days before Lincoln's inauguration, the *New York Illustrated News* of March 2, 1861, made the first official announcement of the beard:

> Now that kings, statesmen, and even handsome priests, whilst preaching of heavenly glories in general, and of their own glories in particular, have adopted the patriarchal fashion of beards and whiskers, as their highest and manliest adornment, there is no wonder that ambitious Americans—desirous of emulating such distinguished company—should cultivate their "mustaches" and "whisker-anders."
>
> Our good President-elect, "Honest Old Abe," sets up a brave example in this respect, which all gentlemen, beardless from principle hitherto, would do well to adopt. "Honest Abe" has cultivated his whiskers and looks as handsome now as the best and greatest of his contemporaries. We have the honor of presenting our readers with the first portrait of him taken with his new facial appointments and we hope all patriotic ladies will fall in love with him.

The same issue of the paper ran another article entitled "Hirsute Luxuriance":

Everyone is talking about the newly
grown whiskers of President Lincoln. It has
become the topic of the day. A few weeks ago
Mr. Lincoln's cheeks and chin were innocent
of anything approaching a beard, and looked
as though it was impossible to produce on
them the noble hirsute appendages of manhood.
A young lady of Buffalo, who transferred his
portrait to her scrapbook, accidentally
discovered that her political hero presented
a much more dignified appearance when
whiskers were penciled on his visage; so she
wrote him to that effect. He at once, like a
sensible man, took the hint, and as time was
precious, he resolved to ascertain what hair-
producing preparation there was in existence
which he could most confidently call on.
Accordingly, he obtained a large box of a

*The gaunt features of candidate
Abraham Lincoln are evident in this
June, 1860, photograph taken at
Springfield by William Shaw.*
(Lincoln photo by courtesy
of the Chicago Historical Society).

"stimulating unguent" known as Bellingham's. With this extraordinary paste he soon started the manly adornment which is at present the theme of all classes of society. By adopting this plan Mr. Lincoln has in a few weeks so changed his countenance that all portraits which have been treasured up as representing him have to be discarded as not any longer likenesses. Mr. Lincoln in doing this is wisely imitating the taste and the practice of all the truly great men of his era. We are as a people very properly returning to the custom of the ancients—to the example of the Apostles and their Gracious Guide—to the fashion of men in the first and innocent ages, as well as to their boast in what are styled as the heroic periods. See advertisement on opposite page.

Lincoln's beard had reached full growth when C.S. German took this photograph at Springfield on February 9, 1861, a week before he stopped at Westfield to show Grace his beard.
(Lincoln photo courtesy of Chicago Historical Society).

On the same day *Frank Leslie's Illustrated News* ran the unguent advertisement, but would not sanction the mention of Lincoln's beard in the advertisement.

On March 3 the *New York Herald* carried a full newspaper column on Bellingham's unguent.

The unguent manufacturer profited greatly from the advertisement, but there is no evidence that Lincoln ever used the product or authorized publication of the advertisement or news article. The article erred by sixty-five miles in the place of Grace's residence, nor did she pencil a beard on the picture of Lincoln.

Meanwhile, on February 9, 1861, Christopher S. German of Springfield made the first fully-bearded photograph of Lincoln.

Chapter 8

OLD ABE'S KISS

A huge throng of well-wishers stood silent and weeping in a drizzling rain at Springfield on Monday, February 11, 1861, as Abraham Lincoln spoke slowly and emotionally from the back of the train as it was about to depart for Washington, D.C.

"No one can appreciate my feeling of sadness at this parting," Lincoln said. "To this place, the kindness of these people, I owe everything."

Lincoln continued, "I now leave, not knowing when or whether I may return, with a task before me greater than that which rested upon Washington. Without the assistance of that Divine Being who ever attended him, I cannot succeed. With that assistance I cannot fail." The train pulled away—and Lincoln never returned alive.

The presidential train zigzagged back and forth between major northern cities during a triumphant twelve-day trip from Springfield to Washington. Lincoln's purpose was to be seen by as many people as possible—and to enlist their support. The train journeyed to Columbus and Pittsburgh, then northwest to Cleveland. At Cleveland on February 15, Lincoln marched for two hours in a cold rain.

Then the train headed northeastward along the shores of Lake Erie toward Buffalo. At Girard, Pennsylvania, Horace Greeley boarded the train, had a twenty-minute conversation with the president-elect, and got off at Erie.

Also aboard the train as it crossed the narrow neck of Pennsylvania bordering Lake Erie was the Honorable George W. Patterson of Westfield. His round face, with white hair flowing out from it, was not unlike the appearance of the spectacled Greeley, except that Patterson bore himself in a more distinguished manner.

Greeley appeared before Lincoln in his usual white, rumpled coat, with one trouser leg outside a boot and the other trouser leg tucked inside the other boot. As usual, Greeley also carried with him two colorful blankets and a valise. Those who knew Greeley well were aware that his mentally unbalanced wife had no regard for how he looked in public.

Lincoln turned to the western New York Republican leader and asked, "Mr. Patterson, do you happen to know a family at Westfield named Bedell?"

Railroad depot at Westfield, N.Y., where Lincoln kissed Grace Bedell before two thousand people on February 16, 1861. Photo taken about 1900, shortly before the depot was razed.
(Photograph courtesy of the Lincoln National Life Foundation).

"Yes, I do, Mr. President," Patterson replied.

"While I was canvassing the Illinois vote," Lincoln said, "I received a letter from a little girl named Grace Bedell, in which she advised me, among other things, to wear whiskers, thinking it would improve my looks. The character of the letter was unique, so different from the many self-seeking and threatening ones I was receiving every day, that it came to me as a relief and a pleasure."

Early in the afternoon of February 16, Saturday, the president's special train thundered across the trestle spanning Chautauqua Creek gorge and then chuffed its way into Westfield from the west before screeching to a halt as it came to the depot.

A number of people had left behind written accounts of the events of that fateful day at Westfield. A variety of viewpoints are expressed. First is Grace's own account, written many years later. The sisters mentioned are Helen and Alice; McCormack was Helen's beau; the neighbor providing the flowers was Mrs. Plumb.

I was at the station with my two sisters and a Mr. McCormack, who had escorted us there when the President's train arrived. In my hand was a bouquet of roses, which a neighbor had furnished so that I might give them to the President. The crowd was so large and I was so little that I could not see the President as he stood on the rear platform of his train making his address. But at the end of a short speech he announced,

"I have a little correspondent in this place, and if she is present will she please come forward?"

"Who is it? What is her name?" shouted a number of voices from the crowd.

"Grace Bedell," answered Mr. Lincoln.

Taking my hand, the gentleman who had escorted us to the station made a lane through the crowd and led me to the low platform beside the train. The President stepped down from the car, shook my hand and kissed me.

"You see," he said, indicating his beard, "I let these grow for you, Grace."

The crowd cheered and the President re-entered his car. I was so surprised and embarrassed by the President's unexpected conduct that I ran home as fast as I could,

"I have a little correspondent in this place, and if she is present will she please come forward?"

dodging in and out between horses and buggies, and once crawling under a wagon. Such was my confusion that I completely forgot the bouquet of roses that I was going to give the great man to whom I had offered such rare advice, and when I arrived home I had the stems, all that remained of the bouquet, still tightly clutched in my hand.

It seemed to me as the President stooped to kiss me that he looked very kind, yes, and sad.

Grace also remembered how the famous beard scratched her face, how she was speechless in the presence of her hero, and how flushed her face became when the Great Man kissed her. She did have the pleasure of touching his beard with her hand for just an instant as he kissed her.

When she had gone to the station, Grace fondly hoped that her roses might be passed up to Lincoln, along with other flowers being presented. She had no assurance that he would remember her name. In fact, she feared that the moment of his stop at Westfield would pass without any notice of her role in his life.

She could see from the west the sign that read "Welcome to the Empire State." But dignitaries of the village and county had crowded in front of her so that she could see little of the activity on the train. Her heart jumped when ex-Lieutenant Governor Patterson called her name.

In her haste to run home to her mother, little Grace scarcely noted the rapidly melting slush as she ran across the brick paving of English Street toward the Westfield Hotel opposite the railroad station. She was not even winded until she reached home, after running two blocks, half of the distance uphill along Franklin Street. She took no notice of the sap buckets hanging on the sugar maple trees lining Franklin Street. Her blush turned to tears as she realized her beautiful yellow roses had disappeared, all except the stems.

Grace relived the grandest experience of her lifetime that evening as her sisters and brothers told their parents what they saw and heard that afternoon.

Austin Smith, state legislator and attorney at Westfield, wrote in his diary:

> Abram Lincoln, Prest. Elect of U.S. came thro here on the R.R. today about 2 o'clock. The train stopped to wood and water. He came out on the rear end of the car. After three cheers for Lincoln and 3 times 3 for the Union, he was introduced to the crowd of about 2000 men, women, and children by Gov. Patterson and made a few remarks. He said he could not make a speech for two reasons. First, he was so hoarse he could scarcely make a loud noise. The second reason was that he had no speech to make, and if he had, it would hardly be proper to make it.
>
> "Seeing the large crowd of people, I came out to look at you; and I suppose you came here to look at me, and from the large number of ladies I see in the crowd, I think I have much the better of the bargain."
>
> Little Miss Bedell had written to him saying she did not like the looks of his

picture, and advising him to let his whiskers grow, to which he had written a reply. She was introduced to him, and he jumped down from the platform and kissed her. And pointing to his whiskers said, "You see I have followed your advice."

Writing many years later, Jennie Macomber recalled the event, she being ten years old at the time:

I was one of many who saw Lincoln when he passed through Westfield in February, 1861 . . . His car was the rear one on the morning express going east through Westfield. . . . He came out on the front platform of his car and stood bowing to the crowd assembled.

He said, "Westfield, why this is the home of my little girl." And when she was lifted and carried through the crowd to the platform, he stooped and kissed her, and stroking his beard said, "You see I have taken your advice."

Mr. Lincoln then went to the rear platform of his car and by a rotary motion waved the flag that floated above him.

Another eyewitness account was given in 1933 by J.S. Stearns of Ludington, Michigan:

My father drove the twelve miles from our home to Westfield in a two-horse lumber wagon filled with farmers from our vicinity, that we might see Lincoln and hear him speak. . . .

I remember that he was of unusual
height, having to stoop considerably in order
to get through the door out onto the
platform, and had immensely large hands and
feet. He wore a beard of about an inch in
length, and was wearing what was called in
those days a plug or stovepipe hat.

Charles Stilson, Jr., gave this account in 1928 in
Rochester's *Democrat Chronicle*. The brother
mentioned was Frank, who jointly with Helen's beau
helped Grace up toward the platform. This is the
nephew's account:

On his way to take the presidential oath
of office, Lincoln stopped at Westfield.
After making a short speech . . . he related
the circumstances of the letter, and asked if
Grace Bedell was in the crowd. She was some
distance from the car . . . but as close as she
could get. Townsfolk pointed her out to
Lincoln, and opened a lane to the steps of
the car. Grace's older brother swung the
startled, delighted child up on his shoulder
and carried her through the crowd. Lincoln,
taking a step down from the platform, shook
her hand, kissed her, and said:
"You see, I grew these whiskers for you,
Grace."
The crowd cheered, and the little girl
ran home with only one thought in her mind:
to get to her mother, as the cheering and
shouting had so embarrassed her that mother

and home seemed the only haven. . . .

Lincoln never forgot a friend or a
kindly act; and he had the whiskers as a
constant reminder of Grace Bedell. One can
guess that in his accession to the presidency
and the breaking of the great war, that
laughter-loving man smiled at the memory of
the child's advice and whimsically compared
it with the august counsels of solemn
statesmen, pompous generals, and fussy
politicians seeking to influence to their
desires the penetrating mind and feeling
heart that always gave way to the right, but
were stubborn as adamant against the advances
of wrong.

He wore the whiskers to the end, and
truly that part of the world which cares
deeply for the personal appearance of its
idol owes considerable to little Grace
Bedell.

Several newspapers also reported the incident. The
February 20, 1861, issue of the *Westfield Republican*
published this account written by Editor Martin Rice:

The President-elect and suite arrived at
Albany on Monday. He passed through this
place on Saturday, at 35 minutes past one
p.m. Some two thousand people had collected
at the depot, and a large flag, with an
inscription welcoming the President-elect to
the Empire State, had been suspended near the
passenger depot. As the train came to a

stop, Lincoln appeared on the platform of the rear car, and was introduced to the crowd by Gov. Patterson, and this formed the signal for cheer upon cheer. After quiet was restored he said he was proud to meet so many of the citizens of Chautauqua, but excused himself from making a speech. . . . He, however, continued with a few good natured remarks and put everybody in the best of humor. He then passed to the other end of the car and briefly addressed the crowd in that section.

He stated that soon after his nomination he received a letter from a little girl in this place, making some comments on his personal appearance, and suggesting that his looks would be improved by whiskers, and that having no little girl to answer the letter, he answered it himself, and as the crowd could see, had acted upon that suggestion; and desired that if the little girl was in the crowd, that she should come forward. The little miss alluded to is a daughter of Mr. Bedell, a resident of this place, and is some twelve years of age. She was soon brought forward, and Lincoln stepped from the car, shook hands with her and kissed her, and asked how she liked the improvements she advised him to make. Everyone was feeling so well at this time, and there were so many good natured remarks, that our reporter's pencil did not catch the reply. [Grace was speechless.] After bidding the little miss goodbye and shaking hands with a good many within his reach, the President-elect stepped upon the platform of the car and the train moved off, he bowing to the crowds as it left the depot.

The *New York Tribune* carried the headline:

Old Abe Kissed by Pretty Girl

It was the other way around, of course.

Henry Villard, a reporter for the *New York Herald*, traveling with the presidential train, wrote in the February 17, 1861, issue that the incident took place at the Northeast, Pennsylvania, station, and that he forgot the girl's name in the rush to get to the hotel at Buffalo.

Other newspapers declared that Lincoln's behavior at Westfield was scandalous. Under the head of "Whiskers and Kisses" the *St. Louis Republican* jibed:

> If kissing pretty girls is a presidential privilege, Mrs. Lincoln, who knows her rights and knowing dares maintain them, ought to insist on a veto power for her.

The *Baltimore Sun* pompously declared:

> People of ordinary dignity and refinement are accustomed to keep their endearments for those who have a right to them, and even to these they are offered only in private. But our president calls the

women he likes up to him and salutes them in public.

What is prohibited even on the Paris stage as too gross to be offered to public women, the successor of Washington commits as he progresses to the capital, of which he is soon to be the ruler. It is . . . to be hoped there will be no allusions to the important subject of Mr. Lincoln's whiskers in the inaugural address.

Years later Grace said, sadly, "I never saw him again." But Lincoln remembered her whenever he looked at his bearded countenance. He couldn't help remembering kissing one of the prettiest girls of his acquaintance, brief though it was. Her long, black hair, adoring dark eyes, and sweetly feminine nose and mouth were recalled long afterward during Lincoln's sad, somber war years.

The new president went on to triumphant visits at Buffalo, Albany, New York, and Philadelphia. He raised a new United States flag with thirty-four stars at Independence Hall, honoring the new free state of Kansas. At Philadelphia and Harrisburg, Pinkerton detectives advised Lincoln of detailed plans to assassinate him at Baltimore. Hours ahead of schedule Lincoln arrived at Baltimore in disguise, accompanied by a single Pinkerton detective. The unnoticed pair quickly took a carriage under darkness of night from one station to another at Baltimore, and arrived unheralded in Washington many hours ahead of schedule. That Lincoln was able to disguise his extreme height and well-known face was a major accomplishment. That was the little boy in him playacting again.

Chapter 9

THE CIVIL WAR

For weeks following the warm greeting from Abraham Lincoln on that exciting February day in 1861, Grace had a warm glow in her heart. Her mood was in sharp contrast to the somber mood of Americans generally as the gathering storm of civil war broke upon the nation.

Many Americans felt that war was inevitable. But even in late March of 1861, some citizens felt that conflict could be avoided. After the Confederate attack upon Fort Sumter, voices were still heard calling for a negotiated settlement. After the initial Union military defeats, few people sensed as deeply as Lincoln that a long, divisive, and agonizing civil war was to be America's fate in the next few years.

When Lincoln called for seventy-five thousand volunteers on April 15, 1861, three days into the war, Northern supporters responded vigorously.

On Sunday, April 21, Thomas Macomber, the abolitionist carriage maker in Westfield, wrote in his diary:

> Mr. Mussey, Mr. Warren, and Mr. Drake, pastors of the village churches, have each preached a sermon encouraging the use of force of arms at a large meeting last night to raise men and money to assist the government. More than $1,000 was subscribed to provide for the families of those enlisted. Twelve or fifteen enlisted and eight or ten suits of uniform were promised to the recruits.

On Monday, May 6, Macomber wrote that "a splendid flag was presented to Company C today, costing some 50 or 60 dollars." During the presentation ceremony at the village park that day, a group of young women, including Alice and Helen Bedell, sang patriotic songs from a platform, as a large crowd gathered. Company C, led by Captain Harmon J. Bliss, then paraded around the town, carrying the beautiful silk flag. They carried the flag throughout the war and brought it home. Bliss was killed in action in the war, as was the Reverend Jeremiah Drake of the Baptist Church, who was also named captain of a company he organized.

Grace was caught up in the spirit of this and other

similar occasions. Years later she recalled:

> I well remember how the heart of every
> true and loyal Northerner sprang into a white
> heat of ardor and patriotism at the fall of
> Fort Sumter. Great war meetings were held
> and every soul was uplifted as we listened to
> the impassioned speeches and the grand
> rendition of national airs by the whole
> audience. Only those who lived in that day
> can realize the uplift and enthusiasm of the
> time! And, oh, the grief and suffering which
> followed. I remember seeing a regiment of
> soldiers march away to be taken by train to
> the South. They all looked so young, and yet
> their faces were stern and set with purpose.
> With all the world before them to choose,
> they followed the flag of their country.
> Bands crashed, drums beat. People wept and
> cheered and wept again.
>
> And what a life of torture and anxiety
> must have been that of Pres. Lincoln in the
> years which followed. One who knew him
> intimately said that after a battle Lincoln's
> face might have been painted by a great
> artist and named his most terrible conception
> of Anguish, so full of grief and horror was
> it. In all his pictures one must notice the
> sadness of the eyes.

On July 23, two days after the Union Army's first disastrous defeat at Bull Run, Virginia, the first volunteer company from Westfield went off to war.

They were clad in gray uniforms made by the village tailors. But when the Confederates seized all of the army uniforms in the armories in the South, the Union army changed the color of its uniforms to blue.

A few weeks later Captain Bliss wrote from Camp Caldwell, misspelling Secretary of State William Seward's name:

> Today for the first time, our beautiful flag made by the ladies of Westfield was placed over my tent. About two o'clock we were told to expect the President and Secretary Steward, and soon their party came and stopped in front of my quarters, thinking, no doubt, that naturally such a beautiful flag must belong to the Colonel. By the time Secretary Steward had alighted the mistake was corrected and they proceeded on to the Colonel's quarters and were handsomely received. After review Secretary Steward took special notice of Old Chautauqua. The President was reminded of the little girl in Westfield whom he had kissed. He still carries out her suggestion. He said to the prompter that he was happy to hear from her and would kiss her again if he saw her.

Meanwhile, in July Norman Bedell, his neck now obscured by a new growth of whiskers, completed his assignment at the stove works at Westfield. So the Bedell family returned home to Albion. The Westfield chapter in their lives was closed. Grace never again saw the cottage where she so carefully penned her letter to Lincoln. But several times during the next ten years, as she passed through Westfield on the train, she took special note of the nearly deserted railroad depot.

When the Bedells returned to their old home on West State Street in Albion, one of the first things that caught Grace's attention was a company of gray-coated local militia that practiced marching nearly every evening on the nearby grounds of the Albion Academy. This company of boys had been organized by five-foot-five George Newton Billings, a zealously patriotic farm boy of fifteen, who was named captain.

During his childhood this eldest child of Joseph Drake Billings and Amanda Shaw Billings was very much at home hunting in the woods around his father's farm near East Gaines, six miles northeast of Albion.

George perceived Grace as a pretty young face among a crowd of admirers along the edge of the parade ground. But George was more concerned over the difficulty some of the boys had in telling their left foot from their right foot.

The North had expected that the Union army would easily overrun the Confederacy in 1861, and it was stunned by a series of Confederate military victories. The war dragged agonizingly into 1862.

Dark and portentous were the clouds that hung over the nation when the Eighth New York Heavy Artillery Regiment was organized with volunteers from Orleans, Genesee, and Niagara Counties on August 22, 1862. They were mustered in at Camp Church at Lockport by Colonel Peter Porter of Niagara Falls.

Meanwhile, Horace Greeley respected Lincoln as a man of peace but expressed criticism of his military leadership. Greeley pleaded in August, 1862, for Lincoln to issue a proclamation freeing all the slaves in the United States, including the South. Lincoln's principal motive in continuing the war, however, had been to bring the Union back together.

In spite of his vision, Lincoln was, at times, a careless and inefficient administrator. He had an iron will, though perhaps he unnecessarily gave in to political pressures on occasion. On balance Lincoln was a man of action, who moved more decisively than most other leaders in American history.

In mid-1862 Lincoln prepared his revolutionary Emancipation Proclamation. But his cabinet objected to his issuing it at that time. Following a slight upturn in Union military fortunes in the fall, Lincoln issued the proclamation, making it effective January 1, 1863. Although the abolition decree was limited to the Confederacy—so as not to antagonize the border states—the abolitionists fanned the flames of patriotism anew. Now the war took on a new complexion. Abolition of slavery became the principal issue of the war. Lincoln not only strengthened his position with an important segment of Northern thought, but he also improved the stature of the United States among the nations of the world.

The war dragged on into 1863. In July antiwar riots in New York City lasted four days. Troops had to be brought in from the battlefield to quell the riots.

The North was alarmed when the Confederate army marched into Pennsylvania on its way to New York. But the threat was blunted by the decisive

Union victory at Gettysburg early in July.

Meanwhile, Grace completed common school, then entered Albion Academy in the fall. There she became known as a pretty young lady who learned what was required of her. Her acquaintance with the President was forgotten by others.

On November 12, 1863, just after Grace reached the age of fifteen, Albion and all of western New York was panicked by an expected rebel attack from Canada aimed at destroying Buffalo. The threat did not materialize.

On November 19 Lincoln gave what the *New York Herald* described merely as "dedicatory remarks" at the Gettysburg battlefield.

George Billings reached the age of eighteen on December 7, with his patriotic fervor undimmed. Newspapers constantly appealed to young men to help defend the Union. So on January 2, 1864, George was mustered into Company C of the Eighth New York Heavy Artillery Regiment at Rochester as a private.

On January 23 he went into training at Elmira, New York, remaining there until May 13. Optimism among the troops quickened when General Grant was given command of Union forces on March 9.

"Landmarks of Orleans County," published in 1894, described the movement of the Eighth in 1864 in Virginia:

On the 2nd of June the regiment reached
Cold Harbor. The great battle was in
immediate prospect and this regiment had its
orders to be ready for a charge at 4 o'clock;

but the order was countermanded on account of a rain storm, and night settled down, while many took their last sleep. In the morning the distance between the lines of the 8th and the rebels was about half a mile. . . .

The batteries in the rear of the regiment opened a heavy fire simultaneously with the advance of a charging column, and the enemy replied no less vigorously. One after another went down beneath the storm of iron and lead which swept the plain. As the ranks thinned they closed up sternly, and with arms at trail and bayonets fixed they pressed forward on a run without firing a shot. Down went the colors, the staff splintered and broken, as well as the hand that held it. Brave hands seized them again and bore them onward until the enemy's works were close at hand. Colonel Porter fell, crying, "Close in on the colors, boys!" Major Willett was wounded; a large number of line officers lay dead and dying; one-third of the rank and file were hors du combat [disabled]; a part of the regiment was floundering in the mud; the rebels were pouring in double charges of grape and canister at less than point blank range, sweeping away a score every moment. The line having lost its momentum, stopped from sheer exhaustion within a stone's throw of the enemy's works. All this happened in a short time. The supporting line failed to come up, old soldiers declaring it was foolhardiness to advance under such a fire;

so the brave men of the 8th had to look out for themselves. They began to dig, and every man was working himself into the ground. Every stump, molehill, bush, and tree was a shelter. Thus the regiment lay all day, under the very noses of the rebels, and came away in squads under cover of the darkness. This seemed as hazardous as the charge itself, for no sooner did the rebels detect a movement in their front than they opened a murderous fire of both musketry and artillery. Some were killed in attempting to come out.

Years later George wrote this account of the battle:

It was a damp, warm morning, June 3, 1864, at Cold Harbor. The colors of the regiment hung limp as they stood on our battle line. Blue-clad soldiers, in groups and squads bronzed and war-worn, stood about as an aide from headquarters dashed up and ordered the regiment to form and charge the enemy works in the distance. Quietly, the men fell into line. . . . The order was given and the blue ranks charged forward into the full view of the enemy. They were engulfed in that fire-swept slope in a battle cloud that rolled in upon them from black-mouthed cannon and rifle barrels—blinding, killing, destroying. That night after the battle nearly half of the boys failed to answer muster. . . . It is said ten thousand men went down in twenty minutes. . . . The dead were not buried for days, not until a truce was called and both sides went out to bury their men where they fell.

The Battle of Cold Harbor ranks high in the annals of American military history for its senseless slaughter of men in a futile, direct, frontal assault against heavily defended positions. Filled with patriotic fervor, young George did not stop to question the action.

"Landmarks of Orleans County" continued:

At nine o'clock in the evening the regiment was back in its old position, but sadly shattered. The body of Colonel Porter was discovered on the 4th about midway between the pickets of the opposing lines. . . . The following figures tell the story of what this regiment suffered in that battle: 9 officers and 149 men were killed; 14 officers and 323 men wounded; and 4 officers and 238 men missing.

Throughout May and June General Grant failed in several attempts to outflank the Confederate Army in eastern Virginia. Finally on June 20 the Union forces settled down for a prolonged siege of Petersburg.

In the days that followed the Battle of Cold Harbor George and his comrades lived on meager rations and often drank water from stagnant pools or roadside ditches. George was taken ill with typhoid fever and was sent to Mt. Pleasant Hospital at Washington, where he hovered near death for many days. Many soldiers failed to survive in the shocking, unsanitary conditions of army hospitals of that period.

He was eventually returned to his home in Orleans County to recover. While there he learned first of the fall of Atlanta in September, then of the re-election of Lincoln as president in November, and finally of the Union occupation of Savannah just before Christmas.

Coinciding on November 4, four days before Lincoln's election to a second term, were Grace's 16th birthday and the twenty-second—and last—wedding anniversary of Abraham and Mary Lincoln.

Patriot that he was, George returned to duty after Christmas, transferring to Company I of the Tenth Regiment of New York Infantry on January 4, 1865.

In his Second Inaugural Address on March 4, 1865, Lincoln asked for "malice toward none and charity for all." He called upon the nation to bind up its wounds and "to do all which may achieve and cherish a just and lasting peace." It was the kind of Christian forgiveness that few leaders in history have been able to match. But he, like George and Grace, was repelled by self-righteous religious leaders who were sure what was "right." Lincoln did not belong to any church. His attitude toward the organized church was reflected in his subtle humor. On one occasion while riding in a carriage, he listened to the driver's profanity. Finally he asked the driver, "Are you an Episcopalian?" The puzzled driver replied, "Why no. What makes you think that?" Lincoln answered, "You sound exactly like my Secretary of State, William Seward, and he is an Episcopalian."

Photographs of Lincoln taken shortly after his second inauguration reflected a dramatic change in his appearance from the time he showed his beard to Grace. His face had become gaunt and deeply lined.

Dark circles had developed around his eyes. He ate irregularly, slept little during crises, and had almost no relaxation during the four years of his first administration. Both Lincoln and his wife grieved deeply over the loss of their son Willie on February 20, 1862.

In late March of 1865 General Grant finally succeeded in turning the Confederate flank. As a result General Robert E. Lee's Confederate forces were forced to evacuate Petersburg and Richmond on April 2. George's unit was active in the capture of Petersburg and in the pursuit of Lee's army to Appomattox, Virginia.

On Sunday, April 9, 1865, George wrote to his parents from near Appomattox:

> Marched slowly till noon. We were flankers. General Meade's wagon passed us. They say that there is a flag of truce out for a surrender of Lee's army. Stopped to make coffee at noon when the news came that Lee had surrendered and there was the wildest excitement I have ever seen. General Meade came through at a full gallop, hat off, and yelling like a red man. The boys threw their knapsacks and hats. Officers threw their sabres; the batteries fired blanks and such cheering I never heard before!

But the joy and relief at the ending of a long and divisive war was dampened by the saddest two days in American history. An unparalleled mass outpouring of grief followed the assassination of "Father Abraham" by John Wilkes Booth in

Washington on Good Friday, April 14, 1865. Lincoln died the next day.

Tens of thousands of Americans paid their respects to the fallen president during funeral processions in New York City and Springfield, as well as along the route of the funeral train as it moved slowly across Maryland, Pennsylvania, New York, Ohio, Indiana, and Illinois. The train left Washington on April 21 and reached Springfield on May 3.

The funeral train reached Batavia, 15 miles south of Albion, at 5:00 a.m. on April 26, the day after it left New York City. At Batavia the engine and crew were changed to the same ones that had brought Lincoln through Westfield four years before. The only persons to board the train at Batavia were former President Millard Fillmore of Buffalo and his small entourage. They rode the train back to Buffalo. That Grace was not present is evident from her account years later of all the presidents she had seen—Lincoln, Buchanan, Johnson, Grant, and Benjamin Harrison—but not Fillmore.

Those around Lincoln did not forget Grace. The private secretary of William Seward, for example, sent Grace a macabre memento—a portion of a napkin stained with the blood of the martyred president.

"You were a fortunate little one to receive the imprint of those pure lips," Lincoln's law partner, William Herndon, wrote to her. When Grace heard that Herndon planned to write a biography of Lincoln, she wrote to him about the beard incident. Her letter of December 14, 1866, was quoted in Herndon's book, *Life of Lincoln*.

Sergeant George N. Billings was mustered out of the Union Army at Munson's Hill, Virginia, on June 30, 1865. The war was over for one young man, as well as for the nation.

Chapter **10**

GRACE AND GEORGE

After the war George decided to study business finance at the Eastman Business College at Poughkeepsie, New York. George's seventy-year-old grandfather, Joseph Billings II, a pioneer settler in Orleans County, was furious.

"The idea of going to college is absurd," he growled as he confronted George on the front porch of the elder Billings's spacious, white, frame farm house on Ridge Road near East Gaines, two miles south of George's home. "All you need to do is work hard and live frugally," the grandfather continued, with a sweep of the hand over his five-hundred-acre farm.

George looked his grandfather square in the eyes and declared firmly, "I am going to college."

George's father had also wanted to go to college when he was twenty. His father refused, instead giving him a fertile, nearly level 155-acre farm. But unknown to his father, J.D. Billings cultivated more than the land—a great interest in books, too. J.D. spent winter evenings reading to his children from the classics of the day, much as the teen-aged Horace Greeley had done with his brother and sisters.

J.D. also became a devoted Republican party worker. In 1877 and 1878 he was elected to the New York State Assembly and served as a member of the agricultural committee.

Completing his schooling in one year, in the fall of 1866 George took a position as an accounting and penmanship instructor and assistant principal under Principal Oliver Morehouse at Albion Academy, a thriving institution of more than 350 students, located in a three-story box building near the Bedell home.

As the school year wore on, the red-bearded war veteran found he was not especially attracted to teaching accounting and penmanship to teen-age children. Instead, he was much attracted to one of his female students. By early 1867 the young teacher had fallen desperately in love with the pretty girl who had been affectionately kissed by Abraham Lincoln six years earlier. Grace was now eighteen years old and at the height of her beauty.

Here is the perfect young woman, George thought. About the same height as himself, he was magnetized by her long, black curls, and by a face and figure that seemed faultlessly feminine. Here was a young lady, herself falling in love, who put on no airs, and who was as open and non-obsessive of him as she knew how. She deferred to his judgment—except later in household matters, and in these he acquiesced. She possessed just the right touch of humility and a hearty but wholesome sense of humor.

At the earliest breath of spring in mid-April of 1867, as the couple began to spend much time together, Grace became acquainted for the first time with the unique character of rural Orleans County north of Albion.

The main geologic feature of that area is the east-west gravel ridge that traverses the county about three miles north of Albion. The ridge marks the shoreline of the Ice-Age Lake Iroquois five to six miles south of the present shore of Lake Ontario.

Grace noted that the ridge sloped more gently than the east-west Niagara Escarpment one mile south of Albion. The Erie Canal lay east and west below the escarpment and ran directly through Albion. West of Albion at Lockport, a series of locks brought shipping up over the escarpment to the level of Lake Erie. The escarpment enters Canada at Lewiston, New York, seven miles below Niagara Falls. The falls have cut back into the escarpment that far in the estimated twenty-five thousand years since Niagara River was formed.

An Indian trail had followed the ancient lakeshore ridge for centuries and was first used by the white man in 1798. In 1808 Ridge Road was laid out along this ridge between Rochester and Buffalo.

A unique building material was found in the gravel pits along the ridge—cobblestones. Egg-sized, fist-sized, and larger ones were found. During the period of 1830 to 1860 many distinctive cobblestone houses were built along or near the ridge through Orleans County.

On Easter Sunday, April 21, 1867, as the apple trees were budding and ready to bloom, George escorted his young lady in horse-drawn buggy to visit his family. They first attended services at the cobblestone Universalist Church at Fair Haven on the ridge three miles north of Albion.

J.D. Billings had been a founder of his church, and this was where the Billings family worshipped God in a free and unstructured manner. This approach rather appealed to Grace as well as George. The Universalists believe that truth and righteousness are controlling powers in the universe and that good triumphs over evil. This sect also believes in the supreme worth of all human beings—and that all mankind will be saved. Those were radical views indeed during the 1860s.

On that lovely April day George's buggy then angled east-northeast along Ridge Road to the now-vanished crossroads community of East Gaines.

East Gaines consisted of a cobblestone store and post office on the northeast corner next to the Five Mile House tavern and opposite a white frame hotel, the Perry House, on the south side. A school, a Baptist church, a blacksmith shop, and a dozen houses were also clustered at the intersection. George's thirty-one-year-old Uncle Harlow Billings operated the hardware and general merchandise store there. George swung the buggy north of the ridge, down the sandy slope, and onto a flat area of dark, glacial, alluvial silt loam on the way to his home.

Grace was impressed immediately with the rural grace of the J.D. Billings home, with its large windows and roomy appearance. Several large white ash and sugar maple trees provided shade around the house, but did not cut off the impressive view of the peering gabled north end, visible as one approached from that side.

George's nine-year-old sister, Cora, was the first one out of the house to greet Grace. The Lincoln aura preceded Grace, for the first thing Cora announced was that her birthday was the same as Lincoln's— forty-nine years apart.

Later during dinner the martyred president's name came up again in the conversation. George's father related that during the war he and one of his brothers had called upon President Lincoln at the White House to seek a minor political favor. J.D. was impressed with Lincoln's wit, his patience with visitors, and most of all by the aging countenance behind those whiskers.

The dinner conversation was animated and steady, with Grace, George, Cora, and his parents all taking part. George's shy five-year-old sister, Lottie, said little.

During this and subsequent visits to the farm, Grace developed a great fondness for country living as well as for George. He took Grace on many walks over the farm and along wooded Marsh Creek. They checked the progress of the apple, plum, and peach trees from blossom time to fruit maturity. They watched the growth of the crops—corn, oats, buckwheat, potatoes, wheat, and timothy hay. Later in the summer the happy couple picked blackberries along the edge of the damp woods at the east end of the farm.

As their courtship continued, Grace and George spent much time around the Billings farm and relatively little time at her home in Albion. Grace was attracted more to the strong personalities of the Billings family than George was to the Bedell family. George, however, did pick up from Grace's little sister her "baby" way of saying "Grace." So forever afterward he called Grace "Git."

There never was any doubt in the minds of the Billings family that Grace would become a Billings.

Meanwhile, George was doing some hard thinking about his career. He wasn't anxious to continue teaching at the academy. So when his young uncle Harlow Billings offered him a partnership in his cobblestone hardware and general merchandise store at East Gaines, George eagerly jumped at the chance to go into business. He accepted. He immediately proposed marriage to Grace and she accepted.

The wedding took place at the Bedell home in Albion on Tuesday afternoon, December 3, 1867, four days before George's twenty-second birthday and about a month after Grace's nineteenth birthday. The simple ceremony was performed by the Methodist-Episcopal Church's Reverend Schuyler Seager, a neighbor of the Bedells. Officially witnessing the wedding were J.D. Billings and Grace's first cousin, Benjamin Smiley, of Bowmansville, New York. Ben was also her brother-in-law, having married Alice Bedell.

George and his bride moved in with his parents, a

situation that usually leads to trouble. George and Grace occupied an unused bedroom. But Grace and her mother-in-law proved to be the exception to the rule. Grace was painlessly cooperative in the household, serving as an "older sister" in helping raise Cora and Lottie, just as she herself had been "older-sistered." Grace was simply living up to her name.

Trouble lay ahead, however, although it did not reach a critical state until the autumn of 1869. The store at East Gaines languished for lack of business. Stores in Albion prospered, but the Billings store was too dependent upon the declining rural population and the diminishing traffic along Ridge Road. The railroads, canal, and other roads were competing with what had been the main road between Rochester and Buffalo. George and his uncle also felt the reverberations of "Black Friday"—September 24, 1869—the day Jay Gould and James Fisk, Jr., attempted to corner the gold market in New York City.

Early in the winter of 1870, George sold his interest in the store at East Gaines to Harlow.

Meanwhile, Horace Greeley continued to write "Go west, young man" in a variety of ways in the editorial columns of the *New York Tribune.* In particular, Greeley was promoting a socialistic colony he was supporting at Greeley, Colorado. The bait was out and George bit.

George not only was influenced by Horace Greeley because Greeley was a molder of American opinion, but also through the editor's personal connections in Orleans County, as well as at Westfield.

In 1830, at the age of nineteen, Greeley had stopped to visit a friend at Gaines, north of Albion, for a day. His friend left Greeley at the canal in early evening to await an expected canal boat to continue his journey east. No boat came, and Greeley walked east fifteen miles to Brockport in the dark. That journey on foot and by canal boat transported him from the life of a backwoods journeyman printer to New York City, where he became world renowned as an editorialist and reformer. In fact, as a Congressman for ninety days in 1849, he introduced more reform bills than most sessions of Congress ever handle.

Greeley returned to Gaines in 1850 to visit his sister, Mary Dwinnell, whose house he owned. His mother was also living there at that time. Years earlier Greeley had given Mary the house to live in as a wedding present.

J.D. Billings thought highly of Greeley. Though a Republican all of his life, J.D. actively supported Greeley for president on the Democrat-Liberal Republican ticket in 1872.

Chapter 11

GO WEST,
YOUNG MAN

Horace Greeley was still at it, urging people to settle up the West. When George read Nathan C. Meeker's article "A Western Colony" in the December 8, 1869, issue of the *New York Tribune,* he became fascinated with the idea of going west to Greeley's proposed colony.

Greeley and Meeker expected about fifty families to respond to the article. But when the Union Colony was organized on December 23, Meeker reported that more than eight hundred persons had expressed interest.

On April 5, 1870, the colony's locating committee telegraphed the *Tribune* from Denver that a suitable site had been found on the Denver Pacific Railroad midway between Denver and Cheyenne, on the alluvial fan formed by the Cache la Poudre and South Platte Rivers—forty miles east of the massive Front Range of the Rocky Mountains at an elevation of forty-seven hundred feet in a broad, sweeping vale. Meeker and Greeley immediately jointly purchased twelve thousand acres for the colony. The dream that Greeley had had since his journey to Kansas Territory and points west in 1859 was coming true.

George received the news of the location in a circular from Ralph Meeker, secretary of the colony, on April 14. The leaflet stated that the colony had 444 members. Two days later George received from Colonel John S. Loomis, president of the National Land Company of New York, a circular giving details on transportation arrangements and costs.

On April 25, the first sod was turned in the new town of Greeley, just as George boarded the train at Batavia to join a group of sixty colonists headed for Cheyenne. He sat awe-struck as the Great West unfolded before him. The eastern towns and cities and the farmland cleared out of the forests gave way to open prairie converted to cultivated cropland.

West of Omaha the train entered the tall-grass country, where trees were found only along the streams. Finally they came to the shortgrass country of the High Plains. Later the mighty Rocky Mountains loomed faintly and silently in the west.

All across the grass-covered Great Plains of western Nebraska, George was astounded at the uncountable thousands of bison that blackened the horizon. He shot one of them from the train for the sport of it, as hundreds of train travelers did in the period. In the 1860s and 1870s hunters made a practice of wholesale slaughter of the bison for the tongue meat. In the 1880s profits were made from the sale of the bleached bones of bison killed years before. This senseless slaughter infuriated the Indians, who killed the bison sparingly and used every bit of the carcass. Furthermore, the Indians were soon robbed of their means of survival on the plains.

The colony at Greeley had scarcely begun when the Hotel de Comfort at Greeley became a beehive of dissension. Dissatisfaction with the barren, windswept country spread like poison through the group. George was one of the first to turn away. On May 11 he and others left by stagecoach for the village of Denver, forty-five miles south, at the foot of the Rockies.

During the last week of May, George shook the dust of Colorado Territory from his boots and took the stagecoach on the long, bumpy ride eastward down the Smoky Hill River to Abilene in central Kansas. Abilene, at that time, was the rail head nearest to Texas cattle country, although the railroad had just been extended farther west.

The spring of 1870 was an exciting time to be in Abilene, at that time reported to be "the wildest cowtown in the West." Three-hundred-thousand head of beef were driven up from Texas that year.

Police chief Tom Smith, short and unimposing but exceedingly brave, did a fair-minded job of maintaining law and order in the "Texas Town" that lay between the railroad track on the north and the Smoky Hill River on the south. The respectable part of Abilene lay north of the track.

In the spring of 1870 Smith's deputy was none other than the controversial and legendary "Wild Bill" Hickok. Hickok, with the help of whiskey, showed a hard-line attitude toward the cattle drovers. The Texans hated him for his immaculate appearance and his baiting, bravado attitude toward them. He was greatly feared because of his deadly aim with pistols.

As a law enforcement officer at Hays City, Kansas, and elsewhere, he already had killed a dozen men, all reportedly in self-defense.

Hickok immediately took note of the new stranger in town. He was quick to observe that the young York Stater was unlike the tough Texas cowboys with whom he dealt. The swashbuckling deputy might not have taken further note of George had it not been for the new Spencer repeating rifle he had with him, a

Grace's husband, George N. Billings, 24, when he went west in 1870.

rarity in Abilene in those days. Hickok was fascinated with the weapon.

On a couple of Sunday afternoons in June, George and Hickok held informal shooting matches on the edge of town. This was a friendly competition that both men enjoyed.

Hickok wore his brown hair shoulder length and had a long, drooping mustache. Half in admiration, half by coincidence, George grew his red hair longer and adopted an identically shaped mustache above his chin whiskers.

On a return trip to Abilene later in the summer George was unable to find a place to sleep. So Hickok offered to share his hotel room near the Alamo saloon with George. There happened to be no lock on the door of Hickok's room that night, and no light in the hallway. Before they retired, Hickok spread newspapers on the floor inside the closed door.

Grace Bedell Billings, 24, as a farmer's wife at Delphos, Kansas, in 1873.

"What's that for?" asked George, puzzled.

"If someone comes in that door, I will hear it when he steps on the newspapers, and he will be a dead man," replied Hickok as he lay down on the bed, his pistols and gun belt close at hand on the bedpost. The way Hickok spoke assured George that "Wild Bill" was dead serious. Yet when a neighbor of George's, a mutual acquaintance, walked in the door and slipped on the newspapers, Hickok paid no heed. Again George was surprised. Hickok explained, "I'd know his farmer footsteps anywhere."

The following spring—1871—Hickok was hired as marshal at Abilene. During his eight-month tenure as marshal he antagonized nearly everyone, as the cowhands got out of hand. The respectable townspeople became more and more vocal about his highhanded methods.

Meanwhile, on Monday, June 20, 1870, George set out in search of a homestead. With the rented horse and wagon, he rode ten miles west up the winding, tree-lined Smoky Hill River to Solomon City. Then he swung northwest up the rich, fertile Solomon River valley. It was the middle of the rainy season, but there had been little rain and the warm sunshine beckoned him onward.

Chapter 12

KANSAS
HOMESTEAD

As George Billings rode upstream along the northeast bank of the winding Solomon River on the longest day of the year, he was awed by the untapped riches of the soil in that great river valley of north central Kansas. He noted vaguely the low hills at the outer edges of the broad valley. But most of his attention was on the mighty cottonwoods and the hackberry, oak, and black walnut growth along the river and tributaries.

"Here am I one of the earliest pioneers in this virgin Country," he said to the horse, not realizing at the time that he was tracing the steps of the ubiquitous Horace Greeley, whose presence seemed to be everywhere during the days of Manifest Destiny. Greeley had once traveled up the Solomon Valley, crossing Ottawa County. Camping at Pipe Creek, a tributary of the Solomon River, on May 28, 1859, Greeley had written of the young grass glowing with flowers and of the many Indians and the immense number of bison he had seen.

George's early impressions of the fertile Solomon Valley were best summed up by Editor C.C. Olney in the November 1, 1874, issue of the *Solomon Valley Mirror* published at Minneapolis, Kansas:

> The soil is a rich loam, quite dark, very deep, and just sandy enough to work easily, drain readily, and stand drought remarkably.
>
> Along the streams are wide bottoms from one to six miles wide, not level and subject to overflow like the Missouri Bottom, but sloping enough to drain. These are bordered by gently undulating swells of beautiful land reaching up to the divide.
>
> These are becoming the favorite lands with those who have tried both, as they find they work more easily, and for small grain are better than the bottoms, while for corn they are almost, if not as good. There are scarcely any lands more than 100 feet above the level of the bottom of the river.

The 720 square miles of Ottawa County already had nearly two thousand residents spread over its fertile lands when George looked over the area. But this was nothing to the flood of settlers that soon was to follow.

George stopped first at Lindsey, which held claim to being the county seat by reason of Fort Solomon being located there. This fort had provided protection to the settlers against the Indians during and after the Civil War.

But in 1870 the people of Ottawa County voted to make Minneapolis, two miles upstream at the very center of the county, the county seat. Isaac Markley, owner of one of the earliest grist mills in the state, located at Minneapolis, swayed the electorate by donating thirty acres of land for the county seat. The village site, George observed, was also on higher ground and was better drained than Lindsey.

George crossed to the west side of the river at Minneapolis and gazed in amazement at the array of some two hundred gigantic rounded sandstone concretions on the grassy hill overlooking the Salt Creek tributary of the Solomon. Many of the rocks are ten to fifteen feet in diameter. He smiled in amusement when he was told of the fanciful Indian legends concerning this "rock city."

After a stop at the county seat of Minneapolis, George continued his journey up the river to the tiny settlement of Delphos, located on the northeast side of the river along Henry Creek in the northwest corner of the county.

William A. Kiser, considered the "father" of Delphos, owned the land where the town now stands. When George arrived on the scene, Kiser's house was the only building there. But George found Kiser optimistically dividing the village site into lots. Kiser

also donated a site for a school, a church, and the village park in the center of town.

Levi Yockey, the postmaster and the first settler in the Delphos area, had come from Delphos, Ohio.

Mrs. Kiser was interested in Greek mythology and felt that "Delphos" would be a proper name for the town, because of the importance of Delphi in Greek history. She and others acquainted with Shakespeare's plays took particular note of the beginning of Scene 1 of Act III in "A Winter's Tale." Cleomenes, returning from a visit to the famous oracle at Delphi, declares, "The climate is delicate; the air most sweet."

Except for the wooded strips along the streams, George found the whole valley an unbroken, level, waving expanse of native midgrasses.

Again George looked around. He rode horseback several miles west of Delphos to the crest of the bluffs overlooking the Solomon Valley. Here he stood like Moses looking into the Promised Land, dreaming of future prosperity. In the years to come, he often went to the Bluffs to look with wonder at the "blooming" valley before him.

From the townsite, it was only a five-minute ride northeast for George to arrive at Yockey's claim along Yockey Creek. The dark soil there was deep and fertile. It was indeed a promising land.

Two miles northwest of the townsite was David Mortimer's claim on Mortimer Creek. After George visited there, he rode along the gently rolling, upland countryside, ranging north into Cloud County three miles north of Delphos. He also visited bachelor Del Corning at the dugout on his claim on Pipe Creek to the east of Delphos.

The dugout was a popular form of housing in the early days of settlement, differing from the sod house in being halfway into the ground, often along a slope. The above-ground part was made of sod or logs. The dugouts were warm in winter, cool in summer, and afforded more protection from prairie fires, outlaws, and storms than other forms of housing.

Both Mortimer and Corning were skilled hunters and were well acquainted with "Wild Bill" Hickok. George spent many hours with Mortimer and Corning during the next several weeks hunting quail, wild turkey, deer, prairie chicken, pronghorn antelope, and jackrabbit. This activity afforded George more than a meat supply. It enabled him, too, to become better acquainted with this section of the Solomon Valley.

George learned the details of the Indian raids of 1868 and 1869 from George Shafer, who lived with his large family in a log cabin on Mortimer Creek two miles north of Delphos. The worst raid occurred on October 13, 1868, when three men were killed and several others were seriously wounded by a party of Sioux warriors. The last Indian raid in the Delphos area took place on June 9, 1869. The army secured the Solomon Valley, and the Indians were no longer a threat to the settlers after that time. This was good news to George.

The intense heat and drought of July, 1870, did not deter him from his decision that this was the place to settle. On Tuesday, July 19, after a surprise thundershower during the night, he drove the horse and wagon due north from the townsite. He made deep wagon ruts in the soft earth, ruts that many other settlers were to follow in the months to come. On he went to the upland plateau and pitched a tent three and a half miles due north of Delphos, and a mile and a half north of the county line in Cloud County.

He promptly set out to dig a dugout, and was elated to find rich, dark-brown silt loam topsoil to a depth of about sixteen inches.

George took over a claim to 160 acres filed by Louis Duff two months earlier. On July 27 George rode north to the land office at the Cloud County seat of Concordia and filed his own claim under the Homestead Act to the southeast quarter section of Section 28, Township 8 South (Lyon Township), and Range 4 West.

He chose as the site of his future home the northeast corner of the square half-mile by half-mile farm, along the north-south section line. This was the highest point of the treeless, nearly level farm. The southwest corner of the farm was half a mile east of Mortimer Creek and a mile north of where George Shafer was starting to build a wood frame house.

Living alone, the young war veteran worked diligently to dig a hole about five feet deep by ten by eighteen feet in width and length. He had heard tales of tornadoes and other storms and could see that dugouts had some advantages. But he believed that eventually a frame or stone house would be the only "proper" house.

Later he bought a team of oxen with which to plow out strips of prairie sod to build the upper portion of his dugout home. The door was set into the east side, away from the prevailing winds, while a small glass window was placed in the east and west sides. Then he laid rough-sawed cottonwood planks to form a flat roof. Sod over the top, smoothed out with loose soil, completed the house.

Meanwhile, he sent for his "beloved Git," whom he hadn't seen for three months, to join him at their new home in Cloud County, Kansas.

Grace's mother was apprehensive about her making a long trip west alone. The once large Bedell family by this time had been reduced to three members at home—mother, father, and ten-year-old Eunice. Grace's brother, Fred, had died of typhoid fever at eighteen on the very day George left for the West.

Grace was excited, but unafraid, confident in her own faith in God, and thus confident of her husband and herself. It was fortunate that she possessed this faith at the outset of her new life in the West. Some of the early pioneers of Kansas, on the other hand, were overcome by the emptiness and loneliness of the prairie, and developed a great fear of storms and pestilence. Especially were they fearful of possible Indian attack.

Chapter 13

THE PIONEER COUPLE

Twenty-one-year-old Grace Billings, heading west by train in August of 1870, glimpsed the depot at Westfield, encountered the busy, bustling frontier cities of Chicago and Kansas City, and finally boarded the Kansas Pacific train at Kansas City for the last leg of the journey up the Kaw and Smoky Hill Rivers to Solomon City.

Grace met George at the depot in the river bottom village on Thursday, August 25. Without delay he set the rented team of horses and wagon swiftly toward Delphos. Just as the dry wagon tracks along the Solomon River soaked up the moisture from a recent shower, so did Grace absorb some of George's enthusiasm for "the beautiful and fertile Solomon Valley."

Although she noted that trees were growing only along the river bank and its tributaries, the lack of trees still came as a surprise to her when they left the river trail near Delphos and headed north to the homestead. Except at the Yockey Creek crossing, there were literally no trees to be seen, except at a great distance. Everywhere there was a thick carpet of brownish prairie grass.

She gasped at the openness of the landscape and vastness of the vividly blue sky. For an instant she thought of her childhood angels and imagined them filling the vast firmament, yet invisible to her adult eyes.

Their part-sod, part-dugout home on the prairie appeared to her to be little more than a bump under a carpet. She agreed with George that marauding Indians or outlaws could miss seeing it. An occasional Indian was still seen around Delphos, but they came not as warriors but as curiosity seekers and beggars. As of late August there were still no houses within a mile and a half of theirs.

As George helped his wife prepare over an open campfire a supper of beef jerky, cornbread with sorghum molasses, and real coffee, he told of his plans to get a cook stove.

"But, George, you didn't leave a place in the roof for a stovepipe," she replied.

George hesitated and sheepishly answered, "I entirely forgot about it. But I don't want to spoil that nice smooth roof by digging a hole through it. So we'll put the blamed stovepipe through a window."

When he bought a stove in Abilene three weeks later, he set the stovepipe horizontally through the west window. Since the elbow at the end of the pipe couldn't be turned upward, lest rain come down the pipe and put out the fire, he decided that the pipe had to be turned to the north when the wind blew from the south, and vice versa.

"I almost wore my legs out running up and down the dugout steps adjusting the stovepipe to the changing wind," Grace recalled later.

Space was limited inside the dugout, although they had little really "civilized" furniture at first. The bed, for example, consisted of a straw mattress and buffalo robes on some cottonwood planks. But the weather was pleasant that fall, and they didn't mind being without the niceties of the East. Grace became accustomed to dressing and roasting or boiling jackrabbits, cottontail rabbits, and prairie chickens. Occasionally they had venison or beef. She soon learned to protect books, dishes, and the food supply from soil sifting down from the roof.

Grace's obituary idealized and simplified the struggles she and her family lived through during the decade of the 1870s:

They were typical pioneers of the type which best exemplifies the glorious story of the winning of the West. Youthful and sturdy, they found nature to be neither ally nor foe; it was rather an impersonal force, which at times seemed friendly and at times hostile.

The early years were fraught with hardship

and in the beginning their sole possessions were their small home and their team of oxen. There were years of drought and hot, dry winds, and cloudless skies, years of scarcity, years of adversity—and at times the struggle was almost too much. But the cycle was complete and there were also pleasant years when the rain seductively encouraged better crops and when the sun brought forth harvests that made these two youthful pioneers smile wearily, grateful and thankful that their unremitting efforts had not been wholly without return.

Between rains in September George was busy plowing with his sturdy yoke of oxen. But most of the fifty acres plowed that fall was accomplished in October when fair weather continued day after day, marred only by the relentlessly strong south wind. Inside the dugout they could scarcely tell the wind was blowing.

In mid-October George hand planted ten acres of winter wheat along the north side of the farm. Other times that fall he gathered firewood along the creeks and hunted for game. Sometimes alone and sometimes with Grace, he fished the Solomon River for channel catfish and Pipe Creek for bullheads.

Along Mortimer Creek and the river they gathered sandhill plums and wild grapes, the only fruits available that early in the settlement of the area. Grace made preserves of the wild fruit.

Late in September there was a stirring of excitement. Samuel Doty and his wife, Delilah, and their grown children arrived from Illinois to occupy the quarter section next to the Billingses' claim, on the east side of the road. The Dotys built a half-soddy next to the road a short distance south of the Billingses' dugout.

In September the first store was opened for business in Delphos. Owners John W. Seymour, Alfred Simpson, and H.A. Easley sold dry goods, shoes, hats, groceries, glassware, queensware, hardware, and farm implements.

What did Grace do during those early days on the frontier? For one thing, she often got out the letter from Lincoln and re-read it, entirely unaware of the great value it would have later. She mended clothes and made feed sack curtains for the windows. She dyed feed sacks purple and made shirts for George and dresses for herself. When it rained, she fought to keep the water from coming in through the door. She also wrote letters to her married sisters, Alice and Helen, and to her sisters-in-law, Cora and Lottie. Mail came in and out weekly by horseback to the Yockey Creek post office northwest of Delphos.

Whenever possible, she worked or read outside, observing the fading glory of patches of wild sunflowers, the flicker of yellow underbellies as western meadowlarks flitted about, and the golden leaves of distant cottonwood trees. Above the south of the wind she could hear the yip-yip of distant coyotes and the honking of wild geese flying south.

George and Grace gave thanks for what little they did have during a meager Thanksgiving dinner on November 24. The next day George and several other men in the area left on an extended buffalo hunt into the upper Republican River Valley in Republic and Jewell Counties near the Nebraska border.

Four hunters rode alongside the stampeding herd of bison for two or three miles, firing their Spencer or Sharps repeating rifles as fast as they could. The herd numbered uncounted thousands and the ground trembled half a mile away during a stampede. A good shot would stop one of the animals dead in its tracks, as the rest of the herd thundered on past the writhing form. Five other men followed, skinning the buffalo for their hides. Usually the only meat saved was the tongue and liver, plus the tallow. Sometimes a hind quarter of a young animal was salvaged for winter food supply. Later another crew came along and gathered up the hides and hauled them by wagon to the railroad at Salina, fourteen miles up the Smoky Hill River west of Solomon City.

For a week before Christmas and two weeks afterward, the Delphos pioneers were locked in the grip of winter weather more severe than Grace and George had ever experienced. Their little dugout, however, was surprisingly comfortable inside.

Chapter 14

NEW NEIGHBORS

More severe winter weather, with snow up to a foot deep, tested the Billingses' stamina during mid-January and early February of 1871. But by the end of February the promise of spring descended upon them. The healthy, bright green winter wheat crop was an especially promising sign. The purchase of a bred dairy heifer and a few hens and roosters lifted Grace's spirits. Full of optimism, George went out to the fields almost daily during March to prepare the seedbed and to plant oats and potatoes.

Best of all were the new neighbors who moved into their area. The procession started with Joe McIntire and his wife, Ellen, and infant daughter, who arrived in March to establish a claim three-quarters of a mile northeast. Ellen was a roly-poly, warm-hearted woman with a hearty laugh and an easy sense of humor. Ellie set the tone for their circle of close friends, which included George and Alice Nichols, Will and Allie Webster, and George and Grace. They were a jolly set of young married couples who didn't take life as seriously as some settlers did.

Will Webster and George Nichols, along with George Billings, were called the "York Staters" or part of the "Colorado crew," having come from western New York by way of Greeley, Colorado.

Will and Allie filed a claim on the quarter section immediately north of the Billings claim, and built their sod house a quarter mile north of the Billings dugout.

George and Alice Nichols filed claims on 80 acres west and 80 east of the road to Delphos just north of the county line. They promptly built a frame house, which today is the oldest house in that vicinity.

Will and George Billings remained close friends for the rest of Will's life. He enjoyed hunting and fishing, but was not especially skilled at farming. Short of stature, he seemed to hunker down under Allie's "henpecking."

The distinguished looking George Nichols became a successful farmer and served a term in the state legislature in 1876.

Other families moved in around this nucleus during 1871. Nearest to the Billingses were Enric and Jane Packard from Illinois and their two little girls. Enric built a sod house just a half mile south. He was a huge hulk of a man, with the strength of a mule. His sorghum mill attracted neighbors to his farm when they had sorghum to make into syrup. Jane was scarcely more than half the size of her husband.

Two incidents involving Grace that spring had her friends chuckling for weeks. One evening when George returned home from Delphos, Grace complained about the three big dogs that were hanging around the chicken coop.

"I had to chase them away with a broom," she said.

George thought for a moment, trying to figure out whose dogs they might be. "What did they look like?" he asked.

"Oh, they were dark gray and had pointed ears, big heads and feet, and long, bushy tails," she replied, weighing each word carefully.

George's face turned pale, "Oh my God, Git," he shouted. "Don't you realize what they were! They were timber wolves.

"No one in his right mind would take after a pack of wolves with only a broom!"

On another occasion George butchered a young pig. Then he gave directions to his wife, "The way to remove the pig's hair is to hold it by the tail and dip the pig in a large pot of boiling water, and sozzle it up and down; then take a knife and scrape the hair off."

When she took the pig carcass by the tail, it slipped out of her hands into the boiling water. When she pulled it back up, the skin came off the tail. She was so surprised she screamed and nearly fainted.

It was a busy April and May for George as he harrowed the plowed ground and then planted corn, sorghum, and beans—mostly corn. He also began building a frame house over their dugout. He had plenty of help with his building project from his "York State" friends, and he helped them with building and threshing.

Meanwhile, the village of Delphos was growing rapidly. T.F. Beaver built a dam on the river half a mile south of the village square and built a flour mill and sawmill there in partnership with Kiser and Simpson. Levi Yockey built the Delphos Hotel next to the village square; it became the Disney Hotel the next year when L.S. Disney bought it. George Strickler built a store and post office during the previous winter, with mail delivery to the office increasing to three times a week by late summer.

The ninety-fifth anniversary of the United States on July 4 was celebrated with great interest. Strickler, also a columnist for the *Delphos Herald*, wrote of the 1871 celebration:

> Among other things, swings were erected, which were left at the place, and afterwards created much wonder and curiosity by the Indians who visited the scene.

On July 11 George wrote to his parents:

> Grace has five hens and 25 chickens and wants to know if you can beat that. Grace's courage has improved mightily. She dares walk up to a setting hen if she only has the hoe and pitchfork along and if the hen doesn't bristle. She doesn't mind the pecking, but they look so fierce when their backs are up.

On July 14 he wrote to his parents:

Crops bring nothing and it takes so much
capital to start. All I have for stock I can
put in my eye. Stock pays a heavy percent.
It's fun to farm here. No stones, no weeds,
and such rich, black soil, I like to work at
it. [George was referring to livestock.]

On November 5 he wrote to his parents:

We are entirely out of flour and have
been for some time, and our fare has been
slim. I go tomorrow to lay in supplies at
Salina. . . . Wheat is worth only $1.50 per
bushel, so my flour will cost me about $100,
and that will last till June. I shall try a
hog, too, and get enough groceries to last
till spring.
    The old settlers predict a good wheat
crop the coming year. If the prospect looks
fair I have a notion to send for Doty's
threshing machine.

The day after Christmas George and Grace heard
the crunch of footsteps in the snow—a noise peculiar
to subzero temperatures—and then a vigorous knock
at the door. To their astonishment there stood the
legendary "Wild Bill" Hickok with Del Corning!
Hickok had been relieved of his job as marshal at
Abilene two weeks earlier and had come up to the
Delphos area to do some hunting with his
acquaintances there.

Hickok stayed three days to hunt, then left, leaving behind his horse, saddle, and stirrups at Corning's place. At Salina "Wild Bill" took a train to Boston, where he joined the Buffalo Bill Wild West Show, his law enforcement days ended forever.

Chapter 15

HARD TIMES

"This winter and last have been the coldest within memory here," remarked Levi Yockey, the Delphos area's first settler, to George on a subzero day early in February, 1872. It was the first winter for George and Grace in an unplastered, uninsulated frame house. They covered the inside walls with rags and past issues of the *New York Tribune*, with little effect. Blankets had to be hung on the north wall to help protect the family against the winter winds. A weary George spent much of his time that winter gathering firewood.

In February, however, a business opportunity came to him, enabling him to make use of his college training in accounting and bookkeeping. Seymour, Simpson, and Easley hired George as a bookkeeper at twenty-eight dollars a month. During the busy season on the farm, of course, George was occupied fully with his farm work. His obituary stated:

Here he gained such a reputation for his honesty and reliability that when the partnership was dissolved (1873), he had no difficulty in obtaining work, first with one store and then with another. He bought a saddle horse and rode in from his farm after doing the morning work, arriving often before daylight to open the store.

Due to abundant rains in May and June and favorable weather in August, George had a good corn crop in 1872. But prices were very low. Thus Grace and George were still on "hard times," living at a bare subsistence level as winter approached.

But they took pleasure in such simple things as visiting with their neighbors, watching the grass and wheat ripple in the wind, and seeing the wild sunflowers and dozens of other kinds of less visible prairie flowers burst into bloom. The top of Will Webster's dugout was a mass of wild sunflower blooms.

George finished digging a well forty-feet deep that summer. On one occasion when George was working deep in the well, he asked Grace to hold the windlass and lower him into the well. She wasn't able to hold the windlass, however, and he fell into the well. She had to get help to raise him. With water from the well they were able to irrigate a garden that included, in time, such delicacies as asparagus, rhubarb, and watermelons.

They had the best of many peach trees grown from seed provided by Yockey to many of his neighbors. The "Billings" peach was described in the area as being "a medium-sized, golden yellow, freestone of perfect flavor."

The couple had some less than pleasant experiences, too. Grace's "favorites" were: washing

farm clothes, making soap from wood ashes and hog fat, and flies.

George's "favorites" were: hauling firewood in cold weather, low prices for his crops, high prices for supplies he had to buy, taxes, cleaning out the stables, and men or women who put on airs.

On Monday, September 16, 1872, they had their supreme joy. Grace gave birth to their first and only child—Harlow Drake Billings—at their simple frame house on the upland prairie, with Dr. Jay Payne in attendance. Hard times, somehow, seemed easier to take now that they had a family. Their happy infant son was named after George's Uncle Harlow and father Joseph Drake Billings.

"The Lord giveth and He taketh away," said Grace sadly, as she clutched her baby son when a letter came bearing news of the death of her father of "paralysis" on October 25.

Grace and George were not absorbed entirely in their own personal lives or the wider community of two counties. This was especially so during the presidential campaign of 1872, when the incumbent, Ulysses S. Grant, was opposed by Horace Greeley. The famous editor did not abandon his "Republicanism," but was nominated for president first by a group of Liberal Republicans who could not stomach Grant, and then by the Democrats who saw Greeley as their only hope of unseating Grant. Greeley was one of the earliest presidential candidates in American history to stump the nation giving speeches on his own behalf. Grant said nothing.

George's first inclination was to favor the re-election of Grant because of his military leadership during the late war.

J.D. Billings heatedly wrote to his son:

Grant is completely incompetent, and the men around him are downright crooks.

George parroted the Grant administration's most telling jab at Greeley:

He signed the bail bond for Jeff Davis to get out of jail at the end of the war.

George also wrote his father:

Greeley is erratic and unpredictable. The Colorado colony is an example of his ideas gone sour.

J.D. wrote in reply what George himself read in the *New York Tribune,* namely that Greeley's campaign slogan was "Magnaminity in Triumph." Greeley pleaded that "the people should put the peace of the nation above the resentment of a war that is over."

"I don't think that any letter I could write to Mr. Greeley would do a thing for his queer looks," Grace joked. But in the end she and his father persuaded George to vote for Greeley.

On Tuesday, November 5, Greeley went down to a resounding defeat, carrying only six states. "The boys in blue" had rallied behind their old commanding officer. Loss of the election was the second of three severe blows that Greeley suffered within a period of ten days. First was the death of his wife after a long illness. Then the acting editor of the *Tribune* attacked Greeley editorially. When Greeley wrote a rebuttal, the staff would not publish it. The famous editor was out of a job! When he was presented a gold watch upon his "retirement," he threw it across the room, smashing it.

Although he had always been a human dynamo who required little sleep, this continuing habit so weakened his mind and body that Greeley himself died at the age of sixty-one on November 29, the day after Thanksgiving Day. An agonized nation wept at his passing, recognizing, for all of his eccentricities, that he was one of the outstanding thought leaders of the United States in the nineteenth century. The State of Kansas officially declared that "of all the friends of Free Kansas, he was the most powerful."

On November 30 George went on another buffalo hunt that lasted until December 24. This was the last such expedition by a group of hunters from the Delphos area, for the shaggy beasts had almost disappeared from populated areas.

From Christmas until mid-February of 1873 the settlers around Delphos suffered through the most severe winter yet experienced in north central Kansas. It was so difficult to keep their house warm enough that winter that George suspended a large basket from the ceiling directly over the stove for the baby to lie in to keep warm. But infant Harlow was more active than his mother figured, for he flipped the basket over and landed on his face on the hot stove. As a reminder, he bore a scar on his left cheek the rest of his life.

Late in March, Grace and Harlow made a trip by train to Albion to visit her widowed mother. On April 1 the Bedell family home was sold to the Reverend Almond C. Barrell. Her mother moved to Bowmansville, New York, to live with daughter Alice Smiley for the last fourteen years of her life.

A.D. 1873 was a good crop year. On August 24 George wrote to his parents:

> I'm about bushed, having worked very hard for the past three weeks. I followed a threshing machine for ten consecutive days, changing work to get more done. I'm still owing $1\frac{1}{2}$ days. My neighbors, the Dotys, bought a thresher, and thus offered me a chance to get mine done on time. My spring wheat went $22\frac{1}{2}$ bushels per acre. . . .
>
> This last week I have been plowing and today I can scarcely creep. . . .
>
> This is four years spent in farming and all that I have to show for it is a few gray hairs. . . .
>
> What crops one raises are only an expense. But I can't lie still. I must keep striving and trying. Our weather is very hot and dry. Grace is parching. . . .
>
> Grace has only one good dress and our white clothes are nearly gone. What we have does very well here, but would not do there. Rather than bear the chagrin, we would rather stay here. . . .
>
> What we ask is that manufacturers deal directly with us, instead of supporting an army of middlemen who are of no use, only suck our money like leeches.

George was encouraged by his corn crop. But again events elsewhere were to affect his livelihood. Another "Black Friday" occurred on September 19, 1873, when the New York Stock Exchange reported numerous business failures. This precipitated the Panic of 1873. Throughout the Midwest, farmers were unable to sell their abundant corn crops, and so dry corn on the cob became an important source of fuel on midwestern farms that winter.

Grace and George took particular note of a quotation from Thoreau:

It makes little difference whether you are committed to a farm or a county jail.

THE
GRASSHOPPER
TIME

To the surprise of the Billingses, January, February, and March of 1874 proved to be exceptionally mild. Temperatures in the sixties in January and in the seventies in February were common. A heavy, wet snowfall in December and a few moderate showers during March gave promise of a year of abundance.

April and May were sunny and dry, a joy to George and Grace, who remembered the damp, cloudy climate of their youth in New York State. Yet they had a gnawing feeling growing slowly upon them. It was too dry. Trouble was brewing. However, they found winter wheat better adapted to dry weather than other crops. In time this became especially true of the Turkey hard-red winter wheat variety; seed was first introduced into Kansas that year by German Mennonite refugees from Russia. George was pleased with the good crop of what he harvested.

As the month of July advanced, the drought deepened, with afternoon temperatures reaching 100 to 107 degrees on more than half of the days that month. Not a drop of rain fell anywhere on the Billings farm that July. The hot, south wind raised swirling clouds of dust from the parched fields. George could scuff up several inches of dust on the surface of the ground on his cornfield.

As much as possible, Grace did her housework in the relative coolness of their dugout cellar. They overcame any squeamishness about spiders and snakes in the dugout to place their straw mattress there in order to sleep at night.

Distant prairie fires frightened the settlers as they swept along at racehorse speed, burning grass, cattle, and houses in their paths. The sky turned gray with dust and ash particles, and the sunsets were extraordinarily red.

In late July, reports filtered into Delphos of an excessive number of grasshoppers in Jewell County fifty miles to the northwest. But these reports did little to prepare the Billings family and their neighbors for what happened on Monday, July 27.

After the weird, pink sunset of the evening before, George half expected a tornado, even though he knew it was too dry. So when he saw a peculiar, massive cloud approaching, he wondered if a tornado funnel might dip down out of it. Instead it continued as a mysterious cloud such as he had never seen before. The cloud shimmered with millions of spots of light. The sun was blotted out. Then an unearthly whispering, as of a host of silent angels, accompanied the huge cloud. Grace wondered for a moment if she was going to see those golden angels. Perhaps it was death's angels. George was puzzled by the rustling, for he been told that a tornado came with the roar of a thousand trains.

At midday the answer to the riddle came, as billions of grasshoppers descended upon them and their farm and garden crops. The window curtains were almost chewed up before Grace could close the windows. They had to fight off the grasshoppers at the door and the chimney in the stifling heat. Grace was nearly hysterical as the hoppers crawled through her hair and clothing and pinched her skin. That night George and Grace retired exhausted on their dugout mattress, having sealed the house as much as they could. Hundreds of squashed grasshoppers covered the floor.

The branches of their young poplar trees by the house were weighted down by the mass of insects that stripped every leaf and twig from the trees.

The plague of grasshoppers, or "locusts" as they were sometimes called, remained on the ground for more than a week. During this time the temperature reached 106 to 110 degrees each day. The stored hay and grain for the horse, oxen, three cows, two pigs, and the flock of chickens lasted but a few days. The cows grew thin and stopped giving milk. The Billingses had chicken for every meal in a race against starvation—their own and that of the chickens. The pigs, strangely enough, seemed to prosper, enjoying the flavor of grasshoppers.

Suddenly the grasshoppers took wing and were gone to the south, leaving no growing crops anywhere.

George, Grace, and Harlow were in dire straits. They had to sell one of their cows. George spent most of his time during the next eight weeks searching for food, including hunting for wild game and fishing at the river. George's parents sent money and food.

The grasshopper invasion was so widespread over Kansas that a state relief committee was organized to solicit relief funds. The committee raised more than a quarter of a million dollars. Church congregations across the nation responded to the need by donating many thousands of dollars worth of food and clothing to the unfortunate people of Kansas.

The weather turned a corner when autumn arrived. The autumn season was about as mild and pleasant, with occasional showers, as anyone could ask for. George planted wheat as usual.

But then an epidemic of "spinal fever" visited the neighborhood. On Wednesday, October 28, George wrote to his parents:

> We have had a serious time. Will Webster's baby was taken sick one week ago today and died Monday morn. About three hours after she died Harlow was taken [sick]. And we thought he would die before the day was out. Spinal fever is what ails them. Mrs. Shafer's little one is dying now and last week one baby was buried.

The winter of 1874-75 was especially severe, for the temperature during January and February scarcely rose above freezing and often hovered near zero. George was hard pressed to find enough firewood. It was also a winter entirely devoid of rain, with but a few light snowfalls.

Spring arrived with certainty by the second week of March, as George proceeded with tillage for the spring crops. But the outlook was dismal as the south wind lifted great clouds of dust into the air. The wheat appeared as if it would not make a crop that year. Finally, rains came in late April and early May. In mid-May their farm narrowly escaped a return of the grasshopper plague that again devastated eastern Kansas.

The next winter was exceptionally mild. The ground had not even frozen by mid-January, 1876. George worked part-time as a bookkeeper at the Billingsley and Kiser store where dry goods, groceries, and hardware were sold.

On Saturday, February 5, the Billingses had a glimpse as of the gates of Hell opening before their eyes. They had been experiencing southeast winds of thirty to forty miles an hour for several days. Then, somehow, a spark ignited the dry prairie grass at a point a little northwest of their farm on the other side of Mortimer Creek. The orange flames rose and spread across the prairie—away from them—at express train speed, creating a huge mass of black smoke in the sky. People and animals saw this wall of flame approaching with equal terror to that of an approaching tornado. The settlers took shelter in root cellars or plowed fields, while the only animals to

survive were those that reached the middle of plowed fields. The prairie fire was moving too fast to combat, and many homes were destroyed. Before it burned itself out, the fire had burned over the incredible area of two hundred square miles of western Cloud County—almost a third of the county.

George and Will Webster rode swiftly behind the fire over smoldering ashes with water drawn from wells to try to check the flames consuming houses and sheds. Mostly they could only give comfort to the fire victims. With typical Kansas warmth, the surrounding farm families gave food, clothing, and shelter to their unfortunate neighbors.

A furious blizzard struck on Sunday, March 26, long after spring arrived. George, Grace, and Harlow were terrified. Fortunately, the storm ended the next day. The sun came out and soon melted the snow, benefiting the wheat crop. The burned-over prairie slowly turned from black to bright green.

Late in April, just before he planted corn, George set out more than two hundred slips of cottonwood trees on their farm in a row alongside the road. In time they grew to be large trees, forming a canopy over the road by 1900.

Late July and August rains helped the corn and sorghum crops. But in mid-September the grasshoppers came again. George plowed furrows and burned coal oil and straw in strips in an effort to combat the army marching toward his mature crop of corn. But it was to little avail. Furiously he picked two wagonloads of unhusked corn and piled it in the shed. Next he poured coal oil on the ground around the shed and fought off the hoppers. The sorghum crop, though, was a total loss. The family lived through the next winter somehow, but with only enough food to barely survive. George was discouraged. The Far West beckoned.

Chapter 17

TREK TO ARIZONA

Farming prospects during late winter and early spring of 1877 appeared dismal to George. He and his friends were thus swayed by the lure of good jobs in the lead, zinc, and copper mines at Prescott, Arizona. So in mid-April Grace and Harlow went east to stay at the J.D. Billings home.

Will and Sam Webster and George Billings, all of Delphos, accompanied one wagon pulled by a team of mules. Mert Culstraw, John Hicks, and Dan Robinson of Minneapolis had a second team and wagon. Mr. Isbell and son George of Lincoln, Kansas, had a third team and wagon. George Billings was the leader.

John Hicks, a teacher, was tall, taciturn, and well-read. He was serious when the occasion called for it, but at other times was a unique practical joker. He was a "good guy" western adventurer—so much so that a quarter of a century later author Owen Wister used him as the model for the Virginian in his western classic, "The Virginian."

Hicks's "Smile when you say that, partner," has become part of the legend of the Old West. The baby-switching prank described in "The Virginian" came right out of Hicks's life. The Virginian became the classic cowboy characterization upon which scores of motion picture "westerns" were patterned during the first half of the twentieth century.

The Websters were typical westerners in another sense, taking readily to the wagon train outdoor type of living, not so much as an adventure, nor so colorfully as Hicks, but rather as an ordinary kind of living.

Most wagon trains taking the Santa Fe Trail southwest made the trip during the spring when rain was likely to be more plentiful, thus making the water supply dependable over semiarid country.

As the railroad had moved on westward into Colorado, so had the eastern terminus of the Santa Fe Trail that most wagon trains took. But George's party chose to go all the way by wagon train. They picked up the deep ruts of the old trail at abandoned Fort Zarah at the mouth of Walnut Creek near Great Bend.

George wrote in his diary:
April 24: Cold but clear. Wind in
northeast a gale. Crossed Saline River and

camped for dinner under river brush, where grass fresh and green. We followed Elkhorn [Creek] 14 miles.

April 26: Rain came down so hard we had to halt. . . .Followed a divide trail winding over rolling country to Plum Creek. Walked till my feet were blistered.

April 27: A fearful storm of rain and wind so cold we can hardly keep comfortable. The little brush on Plum Creek affords no dry fuel or protection. Some snow is falling. We have crawled into an old dugout.

On April 29 George wrote to Grace from Great Bend:

Reached here last night. Ice was half inch thick and frost covers everything. The Arkansas Valley is composed of sandy grasses and near the river innumerable sand hills are covered with bushes. The stream is wide, shallow, and filled with sandbars.

George wrote in his diary:

May 3. We harnessed up without breakfast and drove to Dodge City 8 miles. Passed Fort Dodge and reached Dodge City at 9 a.m. Cloudy and cold. Dodge is a red hot town, full of dance houses and desperadoes of the lowest class. At eve we visited the dance houses, each having from four to six girls, and an orchestra. The girls would jump for every newcomer and insist on their dancing, and if the man would dance he must bring the girl to the bar, costing him 50 cents. Some of the girls were pretty and well dressed, but as vulgar mouthed as any I ever saw. One tall, full-formed girl about 20 years old and near 6 feet tall wrestled me; and I used some of my strength. They all had a good natured laugh. They keep the houses open till 3 a.m. A desperate town.

May 7 letter to Grace:

We are 67 miles from Granada [Colorado]. Have traveled through a country destitute of inhabitants for 60 miles.

May 10: Took the old trail for Ft. Union [not through the usual Raton Pass Route].

May 11 letter from Granada:

God bless you, Git. Your letter came from East Gaines today. The whole train waited; they are all harnessed waiting while I read the letter. I have to pull my old slouch hat over my eyes to keep the tears out of sight.

The diary continues:

May 11: Started early without
breakfast . . . no sign of water. . . . Camped on
Two Butte Creek 43 miles from Granada. At
camp plenty of wood, water, and good grass.
The two buttes rise 200 feet above
surrounding country.

May 12: Cool, pleasant morn. Passed
large herds of sheep herded by Mexicans.
Cactus [cholla] 6 feet high and 10 feet
across. Poor grass; barren. Fearful hot this
p.m. Still following Two Butte Creek. Leave this
creek in a gap of the hills surrounded by ranges
on both sides crowned with huge rocks 20 and 40
feet high.

Sunday, May 13: We must up camp, for
there's no grass. Followed canyon for 3
miles, with frowning rocks overhanging on
either side. Dark cedars along crests and in
hollows; we mount the hills at last over a
very rocky pass.

May 15: Driving between Raitoon [sic].
and main range; must soon cross tail of
Raitoon range. . . . Mountains very beautiful,
brilliant in the sunlight. How I wish my Git
were here to see it all. . . . Traveled
alongside the mesa till almost dark.

May 17: Followed a branch of Cimarron 5

miles; beautiful mountain brook; cascades of 20 feet in places. John, Dan, and I climbed Capulin Mountain 3,000 feet. . . . Camped at Kiowa Springs.

May 21: Drove up the Turkey Mountains and followed their divide, having good view of park country below. Camped 6 miles from Ft. Union.

May 24: Las Vegas cursed with smallpox. Smallpox all the way to Albuquerque.

May 26: Turkey in mountains and some deer. We reached Anton Chico on Pecos River.

May 28: Saw a mountain lion last night. At Anton Chico I saw fruit trees. . . . We have been in timbered country for over 100 miles.

May 29: Still driving toward the mountains [east of Albuquerque]. No crops can be raised without irrigation.

May 30: Drove to Rio Grande 15 miles, which looked but 3. Got off road and drove through sand.

June 5: Crossed brook and followed lava beds for 10 miles. . . . Everywhere this side of the Rio Grande flowers . . . are abundant, often covering ground. Upland timbered and valleys grassed.

June 6: Climbing the divide. . . . At noon
we camped without water in an open glade near
the Great Divide. . . . Camped at Bacano Springs
12 miles from the Fort [Wingate].

Sunday, June 10: Commenced down Rio
Puerco, a small stream of red water caused by
rain. . . . Hot and clear. Indians everywhere.
One came in on horseback armed with bow and
arrows and showed us some marksmanship. . . .
Grass eaten off by their stock. No water but
some in holes they make by damming up the
channel of the Puerco. . . . Traveled 24 miles.
Crossed to Arizona. Passed a pretty spring
in a cave of beautiful Queens Canyon.

June 12: We take to sand trails over
bluffs. Hot scorching sand glistening in a
furnace of a sun. Ugly brush. Noon camped 6
miles from Dead River. A terrible country.
Only living things that can be seen or heard
are horned toads, and now and then a yellow
rattlesnake. . . . Drove down to little Colorado
River. No water for 50 miles.

June 15: Rose at 3 a.m. and drove on to
the Mogollon Mountains.

June 19: Plenty of mesquite wood, huge
pear cactus, and many strange shrubs.
Reached Beaverhead about 10 a.m. down a
fearful mountain road, Will and Sam holding
back, I driving. . . . Camped at noon 12 miles

from Verde. Drove to Verde Post 15 miles and
camped overnight.

June 21: Finished the 6 miles up the
canyon and reached crest of Verde Mountains.
Drove over mountain roads all day. Meet many
leaving Prescott. Bad luck for us. Camped
in hills 15 miles from Prescott. Lots of
jackrabbits.

June 22: Drove this p.m. into Ft.
Whipple and Prescott. . . . Both are in a
mountain park and the country quite rolling.
Half of Prescott located in a canyon;
houses stand amidst stately pines.

Sunday, June 24: Taken sick.

June 25. I weighed 168 pounds at
Granada, now I weigh 138.

June 28: Had a bad night; an awful
fever; mouth all parched; tongue and lips
swollen.

June 29: Post doctor called on me. Am
getting better.

Prescott, located a mile above sea level in the Sierra
Prieta Mountains, was at the time the capital of
Arizona Territory. A few days after George's arrival
there he got his first job—cutting firewood at a hotel-
saloon. He had worked there a week before

discovering the top floor was a bawdy house.

Excerpts from letters to Grace:

Prescott, Sunday, July 22:
Dear Old Pet,

I have been at work this last week as hard as I ever worked in my life, hauling bricks. I made the first day with the mules $4, the next $8, and yesterday Will and I made $11, but out of this comes our grub. We cook it ourselves. . . . If Will and I can get work right along, I shall send you money.

Prescott, Wednesday, August 1:

I am out of a job now and likely to be for some time. I earned in 8 days $72 by hauling brick and wood, but expenses cut it down to $50; this I divided with Will.

Prescott, Saturday, August 18:

I have been busy at work this week.Last Saturday our mules took it into their heads that they wanted to see Kansas and they took the trail back. I tracked them over the mountains and followed them 34 miles in one afternoon, and on foot at that. But I knew that I must overtake them at the start or not at all. Nearly all the road was over lonely mountains and through gloomy canyons. At night I found a ranch and some water. The mules had passed four hours before. . . . While there an officer came from Verde and had seen them 12 miles

ahead. . . . At the ranch they had seen a
mountain lion that day and many large wolves
were about and several bears. I lay down at
the ranch till about 10 p.m., and then
followed the trail by dim light, as there was
no moon. The trail was barely visible. I
had started out with only my pants, shirt,
shoes, and hat, and no arms. When about 6
miles out I was climbing a mountain thickly
crowded with scrubby oak and juniper bushes,
when I heard the sound of feet in the brush
and chaparral to my left. My heart stood
still as I heard it coming directly toward
me. I knew there was no help nearer than 6
miles. I felt over the trail which
heretofore had been covered with loose rock,
but not one now. I could see the dark form
of the animal as he came with bounds directly
toward me. I found my pocket knife and
opened the broken pointed blade and made up
my mind that now I must die. The animal
halted 10 feet from me and crouched ready for
a spring. With knife in hand I started for
him and gave a yell that was fearful. I
never heard my voice sound so before. The
only move was a lowering crouch and muttering
growls and snarls, but he would not run; so
we both stood facing each other at six feet. I
was scared. I yelled again, and then way off
in the bush, a Mexican began calling off his
dog, and that was the first time I knew it
was a dog. The dog was bound to bite me
though and followed me 40 rods, jumping at my

back. A herd of deer bounded out close by and I was as badly scared as at the dog. I found the mules about midnight at a ranch only a few miles from Verde. The man was a gentleman and made me a bed and the next morning furnished me with a good breakfast free and a saddle to ride to Prescott in. On my way back I saw my friend of the night before. He was a very large dog, yellow with cropped ears, and a head all covered with scars and wounds.

Delphos, Friday, November 2, 1877:
    We came in yesterday during a northwest storm of wind and rain, and I must say the country looked poor and sickly; it does not look half as well as I thought it would. They had a very wet season and the country is covered with an enormous growth of tall grass and it looks swampy and wet.

In 1910 George recalled the 1877 trip to Arizona and the winter that followed:

    We traveled near 3,000 miles that summer with mules and wagon, one of our party driving in turn while the other two walked. We passed through the Indian tribes, Pueblos and Navajos, over long, dry trails, and many times without water, for nearly 100 miles, to find when we reached our destination that times were hard, and provisions and feed high, with employment at any price hard to find.

Early in September we started homeward for Kansas, stopping in the Mogollon Mountains long enough to shoot deer and "jerk" venison for food on the long trail home.

In October we reached Trinidad, Colo., and while on the Great Plains we encountered a snowstorm and nearly a foot in depth lay on the ground. Our clothing was nearly worn out, and our shoes were full of holes; one drove; two walked with the snow water sloshing from our shoes. It was cold and ice formed at night; there was no hay and no grass, but we kept on until we reached Las Animas and the railroad, and food and shelter for man and beast. We reached Kansas in late October during a cold rainstorm and found wet weather and trails all the way home.

Then the wet winter set in, the wettest in the 40 years of my residence here. It rained almost daily; mists and fog hovered about day and night; occasionally snow fell softly in huge, damp flakes. The sun was obscured and it barely froze all that winter.

The creeks were deep, running streams. . . . The wheat which followed in 1878 was the best all-around crop we have ever known.

Chapter 18

NEW ENTERPRISES

George and Grace had a happy reunion at the Salina railroad depot on December 8, 1877. George observed that his bride was beginning to put on a little weight. Grace, for her part, faced a thinner, but muscular, weatherbeaten husband, who was now much more heavily bearded than Lincoln had ever been. George's beard, in fact, reached to his chest in the style of the incumbent President Rutherford B. Hayes. Hayes had the longest of all presidential beards, but George's was "hairs" longer.

A few days later George was hired as a bookkeeper at the Seymour and White general store, a job he held for the next thirty-three months. As part of the terms of employment, he was given "thirty days of vacation a year to pursue the sports of hunting and fishing." On their first vacation, in 1878, George and Grace camped in the Rocky Mountains in Colorado. During the 1880s and 1890s George was a contributing editor to the sportsman's magazine, *American Field and Forest and Stream*.

But during the winter of 1877-78 the Billingses lived mainly on beans and dried fruit Grace had brought from New York State. Wild game was no longer as plentiful in the Delphos area as it had once been.

On June 1, 1878, George and Grace received Homestead Certificate No. 5176, signed by President Hayes. They now owned the farm!

Progress was on the way. The first passenger train reached Minneapolis on July 4, as the construction of the Solomon Valley Branch of the Kansas Pacific Railroad inched its way up the valley toward Delphos and Beloit.

In June George realized a dream he had nursed for several years. His Uncle William Billings in Orleans County, New York, shipped him a hundred fine-wooled Merino lambs. George then hired a sheepherder who rode horseback to handle the flock. By the next year little Harlow was helping. George made a reasonable profit from his sheep in 1879, but lost money in 1880.

In the fall of 1878, for the first time in more than a dozen years, Grace was sought out as "Lincoln's little girl." John Carroll Powers, custodian of the Lincoln Monument at Springfield, wrote to former Lieutenant Governor George W. Patterson, the Lincoln host at

Westfield, seeking an interview with Grace. With some difficulty, Patterson managed to learn that Grace lived at Delphos, Kansas, but was visiting at East Gaines, New York. Nevertheless, Grace replied to Powers on October 2, 1878. The result was an article published in the Chicago *Inter-Ocean*, the first newspaper account of the Lincoln beard incident ever published quoting Grace.

The prospect of the railroad reaching Delphos stimulated a substantial building boom in the village during the fall of 1878, bringing the population of the village to 235 souls by January 1, 1879. The railroad finally reached Delphos in March. The next month John Seymour, John Correll, and George went into a partnership in a grain elevator in the thriving community. George then divided his time between the store, farm, and elevator.

Strong winds came up early in the morning of Friday, May 30, 1879. Thunderstorm clouds built up

Harlow D. Billings, 10, the only child of George and Grace Billings, in 1882.

during the day so that by mid-afternoon a huge mass of white, billowing clouds could be seen to the east of the Billings farm home. The clouds were so brilliantly lighted by the sun that Grace's eyes could not dwell upon them. She sensed nothing amiss.

George and Grace had been trying to teach six-year-old Harlow not to fight with the other little boys at Bernard School, a half mile east and a quarter mile south of their house. But on this Friday afternoon, Harlow came home covered with dirt, his face and arms badly scraped, and his clothes torn.

"How many times have I told you not to fight with the other boys?" Grace admonished her son.

"But, Mama, a cyclone picked me up on the way home from school. It rolled me and dumped me in some weeds. I'm all scratched up," cried Harlow in a frightened, quivering voice.

"We had no such thing, Harlow. You're going to get a good licking, not only for fighting, but for making matters worse by telling me such a big fib," Grace replied angrily.

Just as she reached for a paddle to spank him, neighbor Ellen McIntire came by.

"Why, Harlow looks as dirty and scraped up as if he had gone through the tornado that just passed east of our place," she cried out when she saw the paddle. "There was some stock killed near us, and some people hurt."

Grace was stunned, unable to comprehend that she had known nothing about the tornado, even though she was aware of the slight knoll between the Billings house and the school.

When George came home from town he found fish

dropped by the tornado floundering in the road south of their house. People in Delphos had seen a huge funnel coming up out of the river south of town, carrying mud and water, and heading northeast.

The *Delphos Herald* of May 30 reported:

> About half-past three o'clock this p.m. a storm of fearful violence passed over this neighborhood, barely escaping Delphos, and leaving in its track death, desolation, and ruin. During the morning and particularly toward the time the storm burst, the sky became dark and the clouds gave sign of rain; it did rain a little, and then the hail commenced, and was as large as an egg; and the tornado came slow, but sure, in the direction of Delphos; then men's hearts failed. Fortunately the storm seemed to make a change and passed on the east side of town.
>
> It roared like thunder, and made desert wherever it passed; large numbers of houses were completely destroyed. We think the violence of it extended 15 miles and the breadth about one mile.
>
> At [George] Krone's place 3 miles [southeast] from town, everything was torn to pieces; the very bark was rent from the trees.

Krone was killed and several members of the family severely injured when the tornado threw them into a barbed wire fence. Many people whose homes were badly damaged were at a Decoration Day picnic west of town.

Tornadoes that day and the day before in Kansas killed about forty people, with the Delphos vicinity one of the hardest hit areas.

The contention between cold air from Canada and warm, moist air from the Gulf of Mexico was unusually strong that spring, for on Tuesday, June 10, a tornado made a direct hit upon the village of Delphos, destroying thirty-three buildings. The village's social center, the Disney Hotel, on the southeast corner was the only building among those surrounding the village square that was not destroyed. The *Herald* office was destroyed, but the stone and press remained intact. Other citizens helped the injured, bleeding editor D.B. Loudon go about the street picking up loose type. He amazed the entire community by getting the Friday edition out on time.

By 1880 the volume of commerce in Delphos had grown so that the safe at Hull's general store was no longer adequate to serve as the village "bank."

Frank M. Sexton, a banker at Minneapolis and Ottawa County Clerk, had a good eye for business. He looked over the thriving community of Delphos and decided that if he could find a suitable young man for a cashier, he would open a bank at Delphos. He was looking for someone who worked hard, paid attention to details, and was of uncompromising integrity and honesty.

Just as George had felt thirteen years earlier that he had found "the perfect wife," so did Sexton in mid-1880 decide that he had found "the perfect young man" for cashier—George N. Billings.

Thus on Saturday, September 4, 1880, the Bank of

Delphos opened its doors on the north side of the village square, with thirty-four-year-old George as the sole employee. He was also a minority stockholder, while Sexton remained a silent partner.

That fateful day proved to be a turning point in the lives of George Billings and his family.

Before long, George realized that he could not properly attend to the bank's business while riding horseback to and from his farm each day. Therefore, in October the Billings family moved from their Cloud County farm into the village of Delphos in Ottawa County. At first they rented a house on the east side of town, and rented out the farm. Then in March, 1881, they purchased a large lot on the corner of Custer and Willow (Sixth) Street, where they had built a large frame house. Grace and George lived there the rest of their lives.

In March, 1885, Grace and George regretfully deeded their farm to Margaret Jaquith.

George inherited many qualities from his father and grandfather, including being a firm believer in discipline. On one occasion when Harlow had failed to put away some tools after repeated reminders, George went after his son with a whip. But Harlow's pet collie, Rob Roy, sprang to Harlow's defense. The dog grabbed George by the leg. George broke free, but the dog again vigorously held him by the leg.

"You cannot be such a bad boy, or your dog wouldn't be so loyal," said George, abandoning the whipping. George himself had been fond of dogs since his boyhood—his harrowing nighttime experience in Arizona notwithstanding.

Through the 1880s and on Grace lived quietly and

gracefully, raising her only child to maturity. She served as the first librarian in Delphos in 1888. She also helped her husband with the ledger at the bank, which had been moved to the west side of the square in 1883. Her brief childhood fame as "Lincoln's little girl" rested easily upon her modest shoulders. No one in Delphos outside of her own family even remembered the incident anymore.

Fame rested uneasily, however, with a disturbed ex-Union soldier named Boston Corbett, who in 1878 homesteaded on a farm in Cloud County, eighteen miles northeast of the Billings farm. During the war Corbett had deserted his post and was sentenced to die. But President Lincoln spared his life at the last minute. Corbett was also held in the notorious Confederate prison at Andersonville, Georgia, for a time.

Near the close of the war Corbett volunteered as a member of a special twenty-five-man patrol under the command of Lieutenant Luther Baker. Their mission was to capture John Wilkes Booth, the assassin of Abraham Lincoln.

The patrol surrounded Booth in a barn near Port Royal, Virginia, on April 26, 1865. The soldiers piled brush around the barn and Lieutenant Baker called for Booth to surrender. At the same time, Baker ordered his men not to shoot Booth, but to take him alive. When Booth refused to come out, the brush was set on fire. During the ensuing commotion, Corbett shot and killed Booth. Corbett later claimed that Booth had a pistol aimed directly at Baker. Corbett felt that he alone should receive the $25,000 reward offered for the capture of Lincoln's assassin. Instead, he received $1,653.48 as his share of the reward. He was furious about being "cheated."

He returned to his home in western New York to become a lay Methodist preacher. But his reputation as the "avenger of Lincoln" pursued and haunted him. Eventually, he could take it no longer. Still a bachelor, he homesteaded on a farm near Aurora, Kansas, where he built a stout dugout of lime mortar. It was more of a fortress than a home. He did no farming himself, but rather used his reward money to pay others to cultivate the land for him.

Corbett trusted no man. The only people he would talk to were two neighbor women. Wherever he went he held a pistol in his right hand, while another pistol was lodged in his left boot. His eccentric behavior at the Aurora Methodist Church during the mid-1980s caused George Billings to attend services there on Sunday. Grace would not go. "I refuse to be a party to gawking at such a pitiful sight," she said.

Corbett sat at the back of the church, with his back to the wall and one pistol drawn. At the close of the service, he edged forward with both pistols in hand and his back to the wall. He laid the pistols down on the pulpit and delivered a short sermon—without an invitation to speak. He then exited the same way he had come forward.

Finally, in 1886, Corbett shot at some neighbor children innocently crossing his property. The community seethed with anger. Twice the sheriff tried to arrest Corbett, but the latter's drawn pistols sent the sheriff away in defeat. The day after the sheriff's second attempt, Corbett voluntarily surrendered. But when he perceived that the trial was going against him, he seized his pistols, backed out of the courtroom with guns drawn, and fled.

He was hired as sergeant-at-arms at the State Capitol at Topeka, a job that lasted until he fired several shots into the ceiling of the Senate chamber. Corbett was captured and committed to an insane asylum. The prosecuting attorney was a part-Indian named Charles Curtis, who forty-two years later was elected vice-president of the United States. Corbett escaped from the asylum and was never seen again, except briefly at Fredonia in southeastern Kansas.

Meanwhile, business prospered at the bank of Delphos. In keeping with his new station in life and the trend of fashion, George removed his long beard, but kept the handlebar mustache.

Then in 1890 President Frank Sexton retired. He offered his stock to George. It was the chance of a lifetime! An excited young cashier hurried by train to see his father and uncles in Orleans County. At first he had no success in borrowing the money. But at the last moment his Uncle Clinton Billings loaned him the money. George returned to Delphos feeling as if he were on top of the world, for he was able to buy the controlling interest of bank stock.

George went on to help found a local opera house, telephone company, and a grain elevator.

Chapter 19

FAME
REVIVED

The years passed, with Grace and George remaining in good health. In her sixties, though, Grace began to be troubled with arthritis, which she blamed on the two broken legs of more than fifty years earlier.

Then on December 3, 1927, they quietly celebrated their sixtieth wedding anniversary. The years had been good to them. The letter from Lincoln was framed and hung on the wall in their library. But little note was made of it by the family or others.

Suddenly, in 1928, and from time to time thereafter, the story of Lincoln and his little correspondent became known across the nation. First came the feature article written by nephew Charles Stilson, Jr., on Lincoln's birthday.

Then Hollywood produced a silent motion picture about Abraham Lincoln that included the touching exchange of letters. The manager of the Grand Theatre at Salina, the trade center of north central Kansas, invited Grace to see the silent film as the guest of the management. Between reels the theatre lights came on and the manager announced, "Grace Bedell, who is now Mrs. George Billings, is present this evening." She stood for a moment, as the audience applauded.

Next the beard story came to the attention of George A. Dondero, a large-nosed Royal Oak, Michigan, attorney. The tale excited him because he was an admirer of and a noted authority on Lincoln, and because he was acquainted with Grace's banker nephew, Levant E. Bedell, of nearby Romeo.

It so happened that Dondero was a friend of Robert Todd Lincoln, son of the martyred president, and of Robert's wife, Mary. Dondero had visited them every summer over a period of years, either at their home in Georgetown, D.C., or at their summer home at Manchester, Vermont.

During the summer of 1928, while visiting Mrs. Lincoln at Georgetown, he told her of the Grace Bedell incident and how he had learned she was living at Delphos, Kansas.

Mary Lincoln's face lit up as she replied, "Would you like to see the original letter that the little girl wrote?"

Dondero couldn't believe what he was hearing! "Do you mean to say that the actual letter is still in existence after all these years?" he inquired, astonished.

"I found it recently among some papers that have been in the family since the Civil War," she said. The two-page letter that Grace had written had been kept by President Lincoln, and then by chance was preserved unknown among other papers by Robert Lincoln from April 15, 1865, until his death on July 26, 1926. The papers were then turned over to his widow.

It was a year before Dondero was to see the letter, for it was kept in the Lincoln family vault at Manchester, Vermont. During a visit to Mrs. Lincoln there in 1929, the Michigan attorney persistently asked for the letter.

"The letter really belongs to Mrs. Billings," Mrs. Lincoln replied. "Take the letter and ask her permission to keep it."

When Dondero wrote to Grace that he had found the original letter, Grace replied, "It seems quite wonderful that the letter written almost 69 years ago should yet be in existence."

A few weeks later there was a knock at the Billingses' front door at Delphos. George Dondero entered the parlor, and bowed to Grace and George in his suave manner. Grace was thrilled to see the letter, but was hesitant to let the stranger keep it.

She noticed that the letter was in a campaign envelope of the type she used; but she was positive it was not the actual envelope she mailed, for it was addressed in an unknown handwriting.

For three days Dondero sought permission to keep the letter, always bowing politely, insisting that the letter would be placed in a "Lincoln museum."

Finally, the aged and ailing George Billings showed the temper of his youth. He shouted, "Here, take the damn letter, and leave us in peace."

Grace was elsewhere in the house and did not hear the exchange of words. She did not learn that Dondero had departed for Michigan with the letter until it was too late. She was furious with her husband, for she had not given permission.

"I really did want to keep the letter," she later told grandson George, "but your grandfather was sick, and I never crossed him. It would have upset him at the time. I am not a fighter by nature, whereas your grandfather was strong-willed."

Over the next few years she laboriously wrote several letters to Dondero, asking for the letter to be returned. She suffered from glaucoma and could scarcely see to write a letter. She had to hold her finger at the beginning of each line in order to tell where to write.

In the meantime, Dondero was elected to Congress in 1932, serving for twenty-four years. He never answered Grace's letters directly, claiming to others that she gladly gave the letter to him. In fact, in an indirect response to a letter from Grace, he spoke at length on the floor of Congress on February 12, 1934, telling of the exchange of letters between Grace and Lincoln and of their meeting at Westfield's railroad depot. Representative Dondero then took the occasion to publicly thank Grace for so generously giving him the letter she wrote to Lincoln. He said:

From the hand of Mrs. Robert Todd Lincoln, he who relates this story received that letter to be returned to Grace Bedell, who wrote it, and through her generous act it has become my sacred possession. I give its content.

After reading Grace's letter to Lincoln, Dondero added:

Grace Bedell Billings still walks among the living. Her temples, like those of the distinguished and honored Speaker of this House, have been silvered by the snows of many winters. She has and prizes the letter Mr. Lincoln wrote her. It is framed and hangs on the wall of her modest home.

The Associated Press reported the incident, in part:

Washington, Feb. 12 (AP) - The strange story of how Abraham Lincoln was inspired by a little girl during the campaign in 1860 to "let his whiskers grow" because he would be "a better looking man" was told today to the House of Representatives.
Representative George A. Dondero of Royal Oak, Mich., earnest student of Lincoln and an intimate friend of Mrs. Robert Todd Lincoln, widow of the last living son of the Civil War President, had waited nearly a year to tell the dramatic story at a Lincoln birthday observance in the House.
The "little girl" who unwittingly was responsible for the famous Lincoln beard was

Grace Bedell, 11 years old, of Westfield, Chautauqua County, New York, when she addressed a childish letter to presidential candidate Lincoln on Oct. 15, 1860.

But today she still lives, at the age of 84 [85], and is Mrs. Grace Bedell Billings of Delphos, Kan., and Dondero holds the original letter as one of his most cherished possessions.

It was a gift of Mrs. Robert Todd Lincoln, who came into possession of it after its years of preservation in the White House. She presented it to him after he had made a special trip to her summer home in Manchester, Vt., to see the letter.

Not satisfied with this, Dondero traveled 2,400 miles more to find the "little girl" and to see Lincoln's reply. He did see it, but he returned with a photostatic copy of the message the President had taken time from his campaign to write, although the election was only three weeks ahead.

Dondero further publicized the story of "Lincoln's little girl" with an article in the July, 1931, issue of the *Journal of the Illinois State Historical Society*, as well as with a full-page feature article in the February 8, 1931, issue of the *Detroit News*.

Dondero did not immediately give Grace's letter to Lincoln to a "Lincoln museum," however. Although he could have sold the letter and made a clear profit, he still had it in his possession when he died at the age of eighty-four in January, 1968. He willed the letter to the Detroit Public Library. It has since been in the Burton Historical Collection at that library, but the letter is not on public display. A copy of that letter, which Dondero furnished, is on public display in the Lincoln home at Springfield.

The most substantial personal recognition given Grace for her bold deed, except Lincoln's personal greeting, occurred during the second week of February in 1930. The February 13, 1930, issue of her county seat newspaper, the *Minneapolis Messenger*, reported the event, in part, as follows:

> Mrs. George N. Billings, of Delphos,
> went to Springfield, Illinois, this week
> [Monday, February 10] to attend the Lincoln
> Day celebration there and be the guest of
> honor of the Springfield Chamber of Commerce
> at a banquet.

Grace Billings in her later years

Mrs. Billings is one of the very few now living who met Abraham Lincoln when he was President of the United States. Further than that she has the distinction of having written a letter to him and received an answer, when Lincoln's campaign for the presidency of the United States was on in the fall of 1860. She was then 11 years old and today still treasures the letter she received then from the prominent man. She is now 81 [82] years old.

The Lincoln Day celebration includes an afternoon's meeting in the old state house where Lincoln made many speeches and a banquet in the Lincoln Hotel in the evening. Mrs. Billings will be the central figure of the occasion.

A Springfield newswoman reported the event as follows:

All this meeting of people, this unaccustomed attention and honor is well-nigh submerging the petite figure of Mrs. George Billings of Delphos, Kans., guest of honor at the Lincoln birthday celebration in this city. Photographers, reporters, Lincoln students surge and buzz around her. It is enough to confuse a much more robust person. But Mrs. Billings's associates zealously shield her.

"You will be careful? Do not make her talk too much or take too much of her time. She tires easily."

And so her interviewer was gracious.

She restrained the many questions that clamored for utterance. . . .

Since arriving in our city, Mrs. Billings has been very busy. Arriving at 4 a.m. Tuesday on the C. & A. railroad, she rested late and then "did the town" by visiting several of our department stores. About 11 a.m. she was whisked off to Lincoln's tomb and this afternoon's program called for a drive to Old [New] Salem.

Every president since the tomb was built in 1874 had had a permanent wreath laid at Lincoln's tomb on the anniversary of his birth. On this occasion Grace laid a wreath at his tomb—perhaps the most magnificent in the nation—along with one sent by President Herbert Hoover. By being placed in the exclusive company of presidents of the United States, she was being recognized as "Lincoln's little girl."

She was also permitted to rock in Lincoln's rocking chair at his restored home in Springfield—the only person so privileged.

Grace was further impressed with the fact that a railroad drawing room car had been sent especially for her to make the trip to and from Springfield.

Grace was also elected to permanent membership in the "Kansas Illustriana" group of the Kansas State Historical Society.

She was happy for George's sake that this honor at Springfield had come to her. George had undergone a gradual decline in his health since suffering a stroke in 1926. Then in June, 1930, he suffered a series of heart attacks.

On Monday, June 23, at 6 a.m. death came to the once stouthearted pioneer and adventurer at the age of eighty-four.

The world grew dark for Grace, as glaucoma brought total blindness to her by 1933. But she was warmed by the knowledge that her small role in American history had been recognized in her old age. On November 4, 1936, she would have been eighty-eight years old. But two days earlier death came to "Lincoln's little girl." The sad event was reported by the *Delphos Republican* on November 5. These are excerpts:

In life, Mrs. Billings was quiet and gentle, with a soft air of dignity, which misfortune and hardship could not destroy. Uncomplaining and courageous to a remarkable extent, she asked for no sympathy, but bravely and quietly accepted her physical handicaps with a smile. She never complained.

Her philosophy of life was one which enabled her to endure misfortune fearlessly, and the Golden Rule of the ages was her guide and inspiration.

Mrs. Billings's health declined steadily since the first of this year. As her birthday drew nearer, the increasing weakness was apparent to all. She passed away on Monday, November 2, 1936, at her home here in Delphos.

Her death is mourned not only in this vicinity, but also throughout a large section of the nation, who were familiar with her childhood history in connection with Abraham Lincoln. Mrs. Billings was known to many thousands as the little girl who suggested to Mr. Lincoln that he grow a beard, and whose suggestion he followed.

The interest of historians and friends of the Great Emancipator in this episode remains keenly alive today, and Mrs. Billings's final years were often brightened by the letters and greetings she received from these people all over the country.

She was laid to rest beside her husband at the Delphos cemetery, located on a small hill east of the village.

Chapter 20

LINCOLN'S
LETTER SOLD

The story of "Lincoln's little girl" did not end with his tragic assassination in 1865. Nor did the story of their special relationship end with Grace's death in 1936. Plays, newspaper and magazine articles, a children's book, and television programs have kept alive the fascinating human interest story.

One focus of interest that was kept alive for many years was the letter that Lincoln wrote to Grace. Judd Stewart of New York City, a noted collector of Lincolniana, sought in vain for years to buy the letter from Grace. His standing offer was three thousand dollars.

For many years after Grace's death, Harlow kept

the letter in its envelope in the bank vault. But whenever individuals or groups, such as school children, came to the bank to see the famous letter, Harlow got it out to show to them. He unfolded and refolded the brittle letter so many times to display it proudly to eager viewers that it broke into three pieces. Not realizing the letter's great value, Harlow put it together again with transparent tape, a practice that is taboo among professionals in the business of valuable papers. He regarded his extensive gun collection as having a greater monetary value than the letter.

When Harlow died at Colorado Springs on August 27, 1964, twenty days short of his ninety-second birthday, the story of Grace and Lincoln was revived again.

Five years before Harlow's death, his youngest son, Roger, had returned from a twenty-five-year career in the advertising business in New York City to become president of the State Bank of Delphos. As executor of his father's estate, Roger was surprised to discover that the Lincoln letter was not even mentioned in his father's will. It was Roger's duty to have the contents of Harlow's safety deposit box appraised, including the Lincoln letter.

He and his two brothers, as heirs of the estate, could not decide who should have the letter. After considering that they lacked facilities for taking proper care of the letter, they decided to sell it, thinking that it might bring perhaps $2,500 to $3,500. A Denver dealer had appraised it at $2,500.

One of Roger's first moves was to write to Dr. Gerald McMurtrey, director of the Lincoln National

Life Foundation of Fort Wayne, Indiana. The foundation, one of the leading repositories of Lincoln papers, had this to say in its November, 1967, issue of *Lincoln Lore:*

> For many years this letter had been retained as the property of the Grace Bedell (Billings) family. It was kept in a bank vault in Delphos, Kansas. The Billings family received many offers for the letter over the years from historical societies, private individuals, institutions, and dealers. The offers were always declined until it was finally decided to place the letter at auction in March, 1966.
>
> In Charles Hamilton's Auction Catalogue, Number 12, the physical condition of the manuscript is described:
>
> "This letter is matted and slightly browned. The center-fold is strengthened with tissue on blank verso, and there are several small tears [letter torn, not teardrops]. Some of Lincoln's writing is smudged, and there are numerous water stains, caused, as Grace Bedell related, by falling flakes of snow as she opened Lincoln's letter."

Grace's three grandsons agreed via telephone to auction the letter. The auction, held Tuesday, March 22, 1966, in the beautiful Jade Suite of the Waldorf-Astoria Hotel in New York City, attracted national attention. Although there were more than a hundred persons present, only one bidder met the "reserve" price of twenty thousand dollars.

The November, 1967, *Lincoln Lore* issue continued:

> The original letter was sold for $20,000 to David L. Wolper, Hollywood, California, at the Charles Hamilton Autograph Auction. . . . Mr. Wolper, a long-time collector of Civil War documents, heads up Wolper Productions, which produces documentary films for television.
>
> This letter, marked "Private" at the top of the page, is said to have changed "the face" of history and it is one of the most publicized in all Lincolniana. It is quoted in many elementary textbooks, and numerous books and pamphlets have featured it because of its human interest aspect.
>
> This is said to be the most famous and valuable Lincoln letter ever to be offered at auction.
>
> In an interview with the press (*New York Times*), Mr. Wolper said he bought the letter "because I happen to be a Lincoln fan. As a collector and from an emotional point of view, it's worth $20,000 to me."

"It was the highest price ever paid for a letter bearing a single signature, and is more than the original of the Emancipation Proclamation brought," said Roger Billings.

"It was a very tense evening," recalled George D. Billings. "Roger and I met David Wolper, then were interviewed on television. In the audience at the auction were representatives of historical societies and museums, as well as Lincoln collectors. When the Lincoln letter was offered in due sequence, its sale was confirmed within a minute. There were no bids beyond the initial reserve by Mr. Wolper. As soon as the letter was declared sold, there seemed to be a noticeable lessening of audience tension."

Meanwhile, on February 16, 1966, Cynthia Wilson, a fourth-grade student at Westfield, wrote a letter to George Love, president of the Chautauqua County Historical Society, on behalf of her class, as follows:

On February 11 for Lincoln's birthday we had a play on the letters Grace Bedell and Mr. Lincoln wrote about his growing a beard.

Then on Monday, February 14, some of us saw an article in the Jamestown [New York] *Post-Journal* telling that Mr. George Billings, Grace Bedell's grandson will auction the original letter Mr. Lincoln wrote in New York City on March 22.

We are writing you because we would like to see this letter brought back to Westfield to be put into the McClurg Mansion [former residence of William Seward]. Do you think that the Historical Society could do something?

One boy in our class suggested that perhaps we school children could help by raising money in some way.

Please let us hear from you about this matter.

The society, of course, was unsuccessful in its efforts. However, Grace's grandson, George, later came to visit the school at Westfield.

Kansas further honored "Lincoln's little girl." As part of the Ottawa County centennial celebration on Monday, August 8, 1966, Kansas Governor William H. Avery dedicated a granite monument to Grace Bedell Billings at the northwest corner of the village square. The heading on the monument reads: "Delphos, the Home of Lincoln's Little Correspondent."

By the mid-nineties the recently formed Grace Bedell Memorial Committee plans to have in place a commemorative statue at Westfield, New York, in Chautauqua County.